A Voyage to the Isle of Love by Aphra Behn

Aphra Behn was a prolific and well established writer but facts about her remain scant and difficult to confirm. What can safely be said though is that Aphra Behn is now regarded as a key English playwright and a major figure in Restoration theatre

Aphra was born into the rising tensions to the English Civil War. Obviously a time of much division and difficulty as the King and Parliament, and their respective forces, came ever closer to conflict.

There are claims she was a spy, that she travelled abroad, possibly as far as Surinam.

By 1664 her marriage was over (though by death or separation is not known but presumably the former as it occurred in the year of their marriage) and she now used Mrs Behn as her professional name.

Aphra now moved towards pursuing a more sustainable and substantial career and began work for the King's Company and the Duke's Company players as a scribe.

Previously her only writing had been poetry but now she would become a playwright. Her first, "The Forc'd Marriage", was staged in 1670, followed by "The Amorous Prince" (1671). After her third play, "The Dutch Lover", Aphra had a three year lull in her writing career. Again it is speculated that she went travelling again, possibly once again as a spy.

After this sojourn her writing moves towards comic works, which prove commercially more successful. Her most popular works included "The Rover" and "Love-Letters Between a Nobleman and His Sister" (1684–87).

With her growing reputation Aphra became friends with many of the most notable writers of the day. This is The Age of Dryden and his literary dominance.

From the mid 1680's Aphra's health began to decline. This was exacerbated by her continual state of debt and descent into poverty.

Aphra Behn died on April 16th 1689, and is buried in the East Cloister of Westminster Abbey. The inscription on her tombstone reads: "Here lies a Proof that Wit can never be Defence enough against Mortality." She was quoted as stating that she had led a "life dedicated to pleasure and poetry."

Index of Contents

INTRODUCTION.

Le Voyage de l'Isle d'Amour, that dainty fantasy which has been so admirably translated by Mrs. Behn, is the work of Paul Tallemant, a graceful French littérateur, who was born at Paris, 18 June, 1642. He was brought up in circumstances of affluence and even prodigal luxury until the extravagances and dissipations of both grandfather and father left him whilst yet young in a state of indigence. He thereupon took orders, but, as was not unusual at the time, devoted much attention to art and literature, becoming well known in society for his songs, ballads, idylls, pastorals, and even gallant little operas in which he never ceased to burn incense to the King. He proved so successful that at twenty-four in 1666 he succeeded to the place of Gombaud in the Academy. His chief title to literary renown at that date was none other than Le Voyage de l'Isle d'Amour. Colbert, his patron, procured for him a pension of 500 crowns, the abbeys of Ambierle and Saint-Albin, together with various other posts affording no small emoluments. Tallemant became a popular preacher and society flocked to hear his fashionable discourses. He frequently counted the Queen and Princes of the blood amongst his auditors. He died of an apoplexy in his seventy-first year. His poems, always neat and elegant, can hardly be claimed to have any great value, although they never fail to please. Mrs. Behn has indeed greatly improved upon her original. Le Voyage de l'Isle d'Amour was first printed at Paris, 12mo, 1663. It was reprinted in Le Recueil de pièces galantes; Cologne, 12mo, 1667; again, 'A Leyde. Chez Abraham Gogat.' 12mo, 1671. Le Voyage et la Conqueste de l'Isle d'Amour, le Passe-Partout des Coeurs appeared at Paris 'chez Augustin Besoigne' 1675. With the sub-title La Clef des Coeurs it was issued from van Bulderen's press at the Hague in 1713, 12mo. So it will be seen that the little book enjoyed no small popularity. The best edition is that in volume XXVI of the collection entitled Voyages Imaginaires, Songes, Visions, et Romans Cabalistiques. Amsterdam, 1788. It is illustrated by an exquisitely graceful plate of C. P. Marillier at the lines

Celui que tu vois si sévère,
Est le Respect, fils de l'Amour.

Him whom you see so awful and severe,
Is call'd Respect, the Eldest Son of Love.

A VOYAGE to the ISLE OF LOVE.

An Account from Lisander to Lysidas his Friend.

At last, dear Lysidas, I'l set thee Free,
From the disorders of Uncertainty;
Doubt's the worst Torment of a generous Mind,
Who ever searching what it cannot find,
Is roving still from wearied thought to thought,
And to no settled Calmness can be brought:
The Cowards Ill, who dares not meet his Fate,
And ever doubting to be Fortunate,
Falls to that Wretchedness his fears Create.
I should have dy'd silent, as Flowers decay,
Had not thy Friendship stopt me on my way,
That friendship which our Infant hearts inspir'd,
E're them Ambition or false Love had fir'd:
Friendship! which still enlarg'd with years and sense
Till it arriv'd to perfect Excellence;
Friendship! Mans noblest bus'ness! without whom
The out-cast Life finds nothing it can own,
But Dully dyes unknowing and unknown.
Our searching thought serves only to impart
It's new gain'd knowledge to anothers Heart;

The truly wise, and great, by friendship grow,
That, best instructs 'em how they should be so,
That, only sees the Error of the Mind,
Which by its soft reproach becomes Refin'd;
Friendship! which even Loves mighty power controuls,
When that but touches; this Exchanges Souls.
The remedy of Grief, the safe retreat
Of the scorn'd Lover, and declining great.
This sacred tye between thy self and me,
Not to be alter'd by my Destiny;
This tye, which equal to my new desires
Preserv'd it self amidst Loves softer Fires,
Obliges me (without reserve) t' impart
To Lycidas the story of my Heart;
Tho' 'twill increase its present languishment,
To call to its remembrance past content:
So drowning Men near to their native shore
(From whence they parted ne'er to visit more)
Look back and sigh, and from that last Adieu,
Suffer more pain then in their Death they do:
That grief, which I in silent Calms have born,
It will renew, and rowse into a Storm.

The Truce.

With you, unhappy Eyes, that first let in
To my fond Heart the raging Fire,
With you a Truce I will begin,
Let all your Clouds, let all your Show'rs retire,
And for a while become serene,
And you, my constant rising Sighs, forbear,
To mix your selves with flying Air,
But utter Words among that may express,
The vast degrees of Joy and Wretchedness.
And you, my Soul! forget the dismal hour,
When dead and cold Aminta lay,
And no kind God, no pittying Power
The hasty fleeting Life would stay;
Forget the Mad, the Raving pain.
That seiz'd Thee at a sight so new,
When not the Wind let loose, nor raging Main
Was so destructive and so wild as thou.
Forget thou saw'st the lovely yielding Maid,
Dead in thy trembling Arms
Just in the Ravishing hour, when all her Charms
A willing Victim to thy Love was laid,
Forget that all is fled thou didst Adore,

And never, never, shall return to bless Thee more.

Twelve times the Moon has borrow'd Rays; that Night
Might favour Lovers stealths by Glimmering Light:
Since I imbarqu'd on the inconstant Seas
With people of all Ages and Degrees,
All well dispos'd and absolutely bent,
To visit a far Country call'd Content.
The Sails were hoisted, and the Streamers spread,
And chearfully we cut the yielding Floud;
Calm was the Sea, and peaceful every Wind,
As if the Gods had with our Wishes joyn'd
To make us prosperous; All the whispering Air
Like Lovers Joys, was soft, and falsly fair.
The ruffling Winds were hush'd in wanton sleep,
And all the Waves were silenc'd in the deep:
No threatning Cloud, no angry Curl was found,
But bright, serene, and smooth, 'twas all around:
But yet believe false Iris if she weep,
Or Amorous Layis will her promise keep,
Before the Sea that Flatters with a Calm,
Will cease to ruin with a rising Storm;
For now the Winds are rows'd, the Hemisphere
Grows black, and frights the hardy Mariner,
The Billows all into Disorder hurl'd,
As if they meant to bury all the World;
And least the Gods on us should pity take,
They seem'd against them, too, a War to make.
Now each affrighted to his Cabin Flyes,
And with Repentance Load the angry Skyes;
Distracted Prayers they all to Heaven Address,
While Heaven best knows, they think of nothing less;
To quit their Interest in the World's their fear,
Not whether,—but to go,—is all their Care,
And while to Heav'n their differing crimes they mount,
Their vast disorders doubles the account;
All pray, and promise fair, protest and weep,
And make those Vows they want the pow'r to keep,
And sure with some the angry Gods were pleas'd;
For by degrees their Rage and Thunder ceas'd:
In the rude War no more the Winds engage,
And the destructive Waves were tir'd with their own Rage;
Like a young Ravisher, that has won the day,
O're-toil'd and Panting, Calm and Breathless lay,
While so much Vigour in the Incounter's lost,
They want the pow'r a second Rape to Boast.
The Sun in Glory daignes again t' appear;
But we who had no Sense, but that of fear,

Cou'd scarce believe, and lessen our dispair.
Yet each from his imagin'd Grave gets out,
And with still doubting Eyes looks round about.
Confirm'd they all from Prayer to Praises hast,
And soon forgot the sense of dangers past;
And now from the recruited Top-mast spy'd,
An Island that discover'd Natures Pride:
To which was added, all that Art could do
To make it Tempting and Inviting too;
All wondering Gaz'd upon the happy place,
But none knew either where, or what it was:
Some thought, th'Inaccessible Land 't had been,
And others that Inchantment they had seen,
At last came forth a Man, who long before
Had made a Voyage to that fatal shoar,
Who with his Eyes declin'd, as if dismaid,
At sight of what he dreaded: Thus he said.—

This is the Coast of Africa,
Where all things sweetly move;
This is the Calm Atlantick Sea,
And that the Isle of Love;

To which all Mortals Tribute pay,
Old, Young, the Rich and Poor;
Kings do their awful Laws obey,
And Shepherds do Adore.

There's none its forces can resist,
Or its Decrees Evince,
It Conquers where, and whom it list,
The Cottager and Prince.

In entering here, the King resigns,
The Robe and Crown he wore;
The Slave new Fetters gladly joyns
To those he dragg'd before.

All thither come, early or late,
Directed by Desire,
Not Glory can divert their fate,
Nor quench the Amorous fire.

The Enterances on every side,
Th' Attracts and Beauties Guard,
The Graces with a wanton Pride,
By turn secure the Ward.

The God of Love has lent 'em Darts,
With which they gently Greet,
The heedless undefended Hearts
That pass the fatal Gate.

None e're escapt the welcom'd blow,
Which ner'e is sent in vain;
They Kiss the Shaft, and Bless the Foe,
That gives the pleasing Pain.

Thus whilst we did this grateful story learn,
We came so near the Shoar, as to discern
The Place and Objects, which did still appear
More Ravishing, approaching 'em more near.
There the vast Sea, with a smooth calmness flows
As are the Smiles on happy Lovers Brows:
As peaceably as Rivulets it glides,
Imbracing still the shaded Islands sides;
And with soft Murmurs on the Margent flows,
As if to Nature it design'd Repose;
Whose Musick still is answer'd by the Breeze,
That gently plays with the soft rufl'd Trees.
Fragrant and Flowry all the Banks appear
Whose mixt disorders more delightful were,
Then if they had been plac'd with Artful care,
The Cowslip, Lilly, Rose and Jesamine,
The Daffodil, the Pink and Eglintine,
Whose gawdy store continues all the year,
Makes but the meanest of the Wonders here.
Here the young Charmers walk the Banks along,
Here all the Graces and the Beauties throng.
But what did most my Admiration draw,
Was that the Old and Ugly there I saw,
Who with their Apish Postures, void of shame
Still practice Youth, and talk of Darts and Flame.
I laught to see a Lady out of date,
A worn out Beauty, once of the first rate;
With youthful Dress, and more fantastick Prate,
Setting her wither'd Face in thousand forms,
And thinks the while she Dresses it in charms;
Disturbing with her Court: the busier throng
Ever Addressing to the Gay and Young;
There an old Batter'd Fop, you might behold,
Lavish his Love, Discretion, and his Gold
On a fair she, that has a Trick in Art,
To cheat him of his Politicks and Heart;
Whilst he that Jilts the Nation ore and ore,
Wants sense to find it in the subtiller W—re.

The Man that on this Isle before had been,
Finding me so admire at what I'd seen;
Thus said to me.—

LOVE's Power.

Love when he Shoots abroad his Darts,
Regards not where they light:
The Aged to the Youthful Hearts,
At random they unite.
The soft un-bearded Youth, who never found
The Charms in any Blooming Face,
From one of Fifty takes the Wound;
And eagerly persues the cunning Chase:
While she an Arted Youth puts on;
Softens her Voice, and languishes her Eyes;
Affects the Dress, the Mean, the Tone,
Assumes the noysy Wit, and ceases to be Wise;
The tender Maid to the Rough Warrior yields;
Unfrighted at his Wounds and Scars,
Pursues him through the Camps and Fields,
And Courts the story of his dangerous Wars,
With Pleasure hears his Scapes, and does not fail
To pay him with a Joy for every Tale.

The fair young Bigot, full of Love and Prayer,
Doats on the lewd and careless Libertine;
The thinking States-man fumbles with the Player,
And dearly buys the (barely wishing) Sin.
The Peer with some mean Damsel of the trade,
Expensive, common, ugly and decay'd:
The gay young Squire, on the blouz'd Landry Maid.
All things in Heaven, in Earth, and Sea,
Love gives his Laws unto;
Tho' under different Objects, they
Alike obey, and bow;
Sometimes to be reveng'd on those,
Whose Beauty makes 'em proudly nice,
He does a Flame on them impose,
To some unworthy choice.
Thus rarely equal Hearts in Love you'll find,
Which makes 'em still present the God as Blind.

Whilst thus he spake, my wondering Eyes were staid
With a profound attention on a Maid!
Upon whose Smiles the Graces did await,
And all the Beauties round about her sate;

Officious Cupid's do her Eyes obey,
Sharpning their Darts from every Conquering Ray:
Some from her Smiles they point with soft desires,
Whilst others from her Motion take their Fires:
Some the Imbroider'd Vail and Train do bear,
And some around her fan the gentle Air,
Whilst others flying, scatter fragrant Show'rs,
And strow the paths she treads with painted flow'rs,
The rest are all imploy'd to dress her Bow'rs;
While she does all, the smiling Gods carress,
And they new Attributes receive from each Address.

The CHARACTER.

I.
Such Charms of Youth, such Ravishment
Through all her Form appear'd,
As if in her Creation Nature meant,
She shou'd alone be ador'd and fear'd:
Her Eyes all sweet, and languishingly move,
Yet so, as if with pity Beauty strove,
This to decline, and that to charm with Love.
A chearful Modesty adorn'd her Face,
And bashful Blushes spread her smiling Cheeks;
Witty her Air; soft every Grace,
And 'tis eternal Musick when she speaks,
From which young listening Gods the Accents take
And when they wou'd a perfect Conquest make,
Teach their young favourite Lover so to speak.

II.
Her Neck, on which all careless fell her Hair,
Her half discover'd rising Bosome bare,
Were beyond Nature formed; all Heavenly fair.
Tempting her dress, loose with the Wind it flew,
Discovering Charms that wou'd alone subdue;
Her soft white slender Hands whose touches wou'd
Beget desire even in an awful God;
Long Winter'd Age to tenderness wou'd move,
And in his Frozen Blood, bloom a new spring of Love.

All these at once my Ravisht Senses charm'd,
And with unusual Fires my Bosome warm'd.
Thus my fixt Eyes pursu'd the lovely Maid,
Till they had lost her in the envied Glade;
Yet still I gaz'd, as if I still had view'd
The Object, which my new desires pursu'd.

Lost while I stood; against my Will, my sight
Conducted me unto a new delight.
Twelve little Boats were from the Banks unty'd,
And towards our Vessel sail'd with wondrous Pride,
With wreathes of Flowers and Garlands they were drest,
Their Cordage all of Silk and Gold consist,
Their Sails of silver'd Lawn, and Tinsel were,
Which wantonly were ruffled in the Air.
As many little Cupids gayly clad,
Did Row each Boat, nor other guides they had.
A thousand Zephires Fann'd the moving Fleet,
Which mixing with the Flow'rs became more sweet,
And by repeated Kisses did assume
From them a scent that did the Air perfume.
So near us this delightful Fleet was come,
We cou'd distinguish what the Cupid's sung,
Which oft with charming Notes they did repeat,
With Voices such as I shall ne're forget.

You that do seek with Amorous desires,
To tast the Pleasures of the Life below,
Land on this Island, and renew your Fires,
For without Love, there is no joy, you know.

Then all the Cupids waiting no Commands,
With soft inviting Smiles present their Hands,
And in that silent Motion seem'd to say,
You ought to follow, where Love leads the way.
Mad with delight, and all transported too,
I quitted Reason, and resolv'd to go;
For that bright charming Beauty I had seen,
And burnt with strange desire to see again,
Fill'd with new hope, I laught at Reasons force,
And towards the Island, bent my eager Course;
The Zephires at that instant lent their Aid,
And I into Loves Fleet was soon convey'd,
And by a thousand Friendships did receive,
Welcomes which none but God's of Love cou'd give.
Many possest with my Curiosity,
Tho' not inspir'd like me, yet follow'd me,
And many staid behind, and laught at us:
And in a scoffing tone reproacht us thus,

Farewel, Adventurers, go search the Joy,
Which mighty Love inspires, and you shall find,
The treatment of the wond'rous Monarch Boy,
In's Airy Castle always soft and kind.

We on the fragrant Beds of Roses laid,
And lull'd with Musick which the Zephires made,
When with the Amorous silken Sails they plaid,
Rather did them as wanting Wit account
Then we in this affair did Judgment want,
With Smiles of pity only answer'd them,
Whilst they return'd us pitying ones again.
Now to the wisht for Shoar, with speed we high;
Vain with our Fate, and eager of our Joy,
And as upon the Beach we landed were,
An awful Woman did to us repair.
Goddess of Prudence! who with grave advice,
Counsels the heedless Stranger to be Wise;
She guards this Shoar, and Passage does forbid,
But now blind Sense her Face from us had hid;
We pass'd and dis-obey'd the heavenly Voice,
Which few e'er do, but in this fatal place.
Now with impatient hast, (but long in vain)
I seek the Charming Author of my Pain,
And haunt the Woods, the Groves, and ev'ry Plain.
I ask each Chrystal Spring, each murmuring Brook,
Who saw my fair, or knows which way she took?
I ask the Eccho's, when they heard her Name?
But they cou'd nothing but my Moans proclaim;
My Sighs, the fleeting Winds far off do bear,
My Charmer, cou'd no soft complaining hear:
At last, where all was shade, where all was Gay;
On a Brooks Brink, which purling past away,
Asleep the lovely Maid extended lay;
Of different Flowers the Cupids made her Bed,
And Rosey Pillows did support her Head.
With what transported Joy my Soul was fill'd,
When I, the Object of my wish beheld!
My greedy View each lovely part survey'd;
On her white Hand, her Blushing Cheek was laid
Half hid in Roses; yet did so appear
As if with those, the Lillys mingled were;
Her thin loose Robe did all her shape betray,
(Her wondrous shape that negligently lay)
And every Tempting Beauty did reveal,
But what young bashful Maids wou'd still conceal;
Impatient I, more apt to hope than fear,
Approacht the Heav'nly sleeping Maid more near;
The place, my flame, and all her Charms invite
To tast the sacred Joys of stoln delight.
The Grove was silent, and no Creature by,
But the young smiling God of Love and I;
But as before the awful shrine, I kneel'd,

Where Loves great Mystery was to be reveal'd,
A Man from out the Groves recess appears,
Who all my boasted Vigor turn'd to fears,
He slackt my Courage by a kind surprize,
And aw'd me with th' Majesty of his Eyes;
I bow'd, and blusht, and trembling did retire,
And wonder'd at the Pow'r that checkt my fire;
So excellent a Mean, so good a Grace,
So grave a Look, such a commanding Face;
In modest Speech, as might well subdue,
Youth's native wildness; yet 'twas gracious too.
A little Cupid waiting by my side,
(Who was presented to me for a guide,)
Beholding me decline, the Sleeping Maid,
To gaze on this Intruder,—Thus he said.

RESPECT.

I.

Him whom you see so awful and severe,
Is call'd Respect, the Eldest Son of Love;
Esteem his Mother is; who every where
Is the best Advocate to all the fair,
And knows the most obliging Arts to move:
Him you must still carress, and by his Grace,
You'll conquer all the Beauties of the Place;
To gain him 'tis not Words will do,
His Rhetorick is the Blush and Bow.

II.

He even requires that you shou'd silent be,
And understand no Language but from Eyes,
Or Sighs, the soft Complaints on Cruelty;
Which soonest move the Heart they wou'd surprize:
They like the Fire in Limbecks gently move.
What words (too hot and fierce) destroy;
These by degrees infuse a lasting Love;
Whilst those do soon burn out the short blaz'd Joy.
These the all-gaining Youth requires,
And bears to Ladies Hearts the Lambent Fires;
And He that wou'd against despair be proof,
Can never keep him Company enough.

Instructed thus, I did my steps direct,
Towards the necessary Grave Respect,
Whom I soon won to favour my design,
To which young LOVE his promis'd aid did joyn.

This wak't Aminta, who with trembling fear,
Wonder'd to see a stranger enter'd there;
With timorous Eyes the Grove she does survey,
Where are my LOVES, she crys! all fled away?
And left me in this gloomy shade alone?
And with a Man! Alas, I am undone.
Then strove to fly; but I all prostrate lay,
And grasping fast her Robe, oblig'd her stay;
Cease, lovely Charming Maid, Oh cease to fear,
I faintly cry'd,—There is no Satyr near;
I am of humane Race, whom Beauty Aws,
And born an humble Slave to all her Laws;
Besides we're not alone within the Grove,
Behold Respect, and the young God of LOVE:
How can you fear the Man who with these two,
In any Shade or hour approaches you?
Thus by degrees her Courage took its place;
And usual Blushes drest again her Face,
Then with a Charming Air, her Hand she gave,
She bade me rise, and said she did believe.
And now my Conversation does permit;
But oh the entertainment of her Wit,
Beyond her Beauty did my Soul surprize,
Her Tongue had Charms more pow'rful than her Eyes!
Ah Lysidas, hadst thou a list'ner been
To what she said; tho' her thou ne're had'st seen,
Without that Sense, thou hadst a Captive been.
Guess at my Fate,—but after having spoke,
Many indifferent things: Her leave she took.
The Night approach't, and now with Thoughts opprest,
I minded neither where, nor when to Rest,
When my Conductor LOVE! whom I pursu'd,
Led to a Palace call'd Inquietude.

INQUIETUDE.

A Neighbouring Villa which derives its name,
From the rude sullen Mistress of the same;
A Woman of a strange deform'd Aspect;
Peevishly pensive, fond of her neglect;
She never in one posture does remain,
Now leans, lyes down, then on her Feet again;
Sometimes with Snails she keeps a lazy pace,
And sometimes runs like Furies in a Chase;
She seldom shuts her watchful Eyes to sleep,
Which pale and languid does her Visage keep;
Her loose neglected Hair disorder'd grows;

Which undesign'd her Fingers discompose;
Still out of Humour, and deprav'd in Sense,
And Contradictive as Impertinence;
Distrustful as false States-men, and as nice
In Plots, Intrigues, Intelligence and Spies.

To her we did our Duty pay, but she
Made no returns to our Civility.
Thence to my Bed; where rest in vain I sought,
For pratling LOVE still entertain'd my thought,
And to my Mind, a thousand Fancies brought:
Aminta's Charms and Pow'rful Attractions,
From whence I grew to make these soft Reflections.

The REFLECTION.

I.
What differing Passions from what once I felt,
My yielding Heart do melt,
And all my Blood as in a Feaver burns,
Yet shivering Cold by turns.
What new variety of hopes and fears?
What suddain fits of Smiles and Tears?
Hope! Why dost thou sometimes my Soul imploy
With Prospects of approaching Joy?
Why dost thou make me pleas'd and vain,
And quite forget last minutes pain?
What Sleep wou'd calm, Aminta keeps awake;
And I all Night soft Vows and Wishes make.
When to the Gods I would my Prayers address,
And sue to be forgiven,
Aminta's name, I still express,
And Love is all that I confess,
Love and Aminta! Ever out Rival Heaven!

II.
Books give me no content at all;
Unless soft Cowly entertain my Mind,
Then every pair in Love I find;
Lysander him, Aminta her, I call:
Till the bewitching Fewel raise the fire;
Which was design'd but to divert,
Then to cool Shades I ragingly retire,
To ease my hopeless panting Heart,
Yet thereto every thing begets desire.
Each flowry Bed, and every loanly Grove,
Inspires new Wishes, new impatient Love.

Thus all the Night in vain I sought repose,
And early with the Sun next day, I rose;
Still more impatient grew my new desires,
To see again the Author of my Fires,
Love leads me forth, to little [A]CARES we pass,
Where Love instructed me Aminta was;
Far from Inquietude this Village stands,
And for its Beauty all the rest commands;
In all the Isle of Love, not one appears,
So ravishingly Gay as Little Cares.

[Sidenote A: Little Arts to please.]

Little CARES, or Little Arts to please.

I.
Thither all the Amorous Youth repair,
To see the Objects of their Vows;
No Jealousies approach 'em there;
They Banish Dulness and Despair;
And only Gayety and Mirth allow.
The Houses cover'd o're with flow'rs appear,
Like fragrant Arbours all the year,
Where all the dear, the live-long day,
In Musick, Songs, and Balls is past away:
All things are form'd for pleasure and delight,
Which finish not but with the Light;
But when the Sun returns again,
They hold with that bright God an equal Reign.

II.
There no Reproaches dwell; that Vice
Is banisht with the Coy and Nice.
The Froward there learn Complyance;
There the Dull Wise his Gravity forsakes,
The Old dispose themselves to Dance,
And Melancholy wakens from his Trance,
And against Nature sprightly Humour takes.
The formal States-man does his Int'rest quit,
And learns to talk of Love and Wit;
There the Philosopher speaks Sense,
Such as his Mistress Eyes inspire;
Forgets his learned Eloquence,
Nor now compares his Flame to his own Chimick fire.

III.

The Miser there opens his Golden heaps,
And at Love's Altar offers the rich Prize;
His needless fears of want does now despise,
And as a lavish Heir, he Treats and Reaps
The Blessings that attend his grateful Sacrifice.
Even the Fluttering Coxcomb there
Does less ridiculous appear:
For in the Crowd some one unlucky Face,
With some particular Grimmas,
Has the ill fate his Heart to gain,
Which gives him just the Sense to know his pain;
Whence he becomes less talkative and vain.
There 'tis the Muses dwell! that sacred Nine,
Who teach the inlarged Soul to prove,
No Arts or Sciences Divine,
But those inspired by Them and Love!
Gay Conversation, Feast, and Masquerades,
Agreeable Cabals, and Serinades;
Eternal Musick, Gladness, Smiles and Sport,
Make all the bus'ness of this Little Court.

At my approach new Fires my Bosom warm;
New vigor I receive from every Charm:
I found invention with my Love increase;
And both instruct me with new Arts to please;
New Gallantrys I sought to entertain,
And had the Joy to find 'em not in vain;
All the Extravagance of Youth I show,
And pay'd to Age the Dotage I shall owe;
All a beginning Passion can conceive,
What beauty Merits, or fond Love can give.
With diligence I wait Aminta's look,
And her decrees from Frowns or Smiles I took,
To my new fixt resolves, no stop I found,
My Flame was uncontroul'd and knew no bound;
Unlimited Expences every day
On what I thought she lik'd, I threw away:
My Coaches, and my Liverys, rich and new,
In all this Court, none made a better show.
Aminta here was unconfin'd and free,
And all a well-born Maid cou'd render me
She gave: My early Visits does allow,
And more ingagingly receives me now,
Her still increasing Charms, Her soft Address,
Partial Lover cannot well Express,
Her Beautys with my flame each hour increase.
'Twas here my Soul more true content receiv'd,
Then all the Duller hours of Life I'd liv'd.

—But with the envying Night I still repair
To Inquietude; none lodge at Little Care.
The hasty Minutes summon me away,
While parting pains surmount past hours of Joy,
And Nights large Reckoning over-pays the day.
The GOD of Sleep his wonted Aid denys;
Lends no Repose, or to my Heart or Eyes:
Only one hour of Rest the breaking Morning brought,
In which this happy Dream Assail'd my Thought,

The DREAM.

All Trembling in my Arms Aminta lay,
Defending of the Bliss I strove to take;
Raising my Rapture by her kind delay,
Her force so charming was and weak.
The soft resistance did betray the Grant,
While I prest on the Heaven of my desires;
Her rising Breasts with nimbler Motions Pant;
Her dying Eyes assume new Fires.
Now to the height of languishment she grows,
And still her looks new Charms put on;
—Now the last Mystery of Love she knows,
We Sigh, and Kiss: I wak'd, and all was done.

'Twas but a Dream, yet by my Heart I knew,
Which still was Panting, part of it was true:
Oh how I strove the rest to have believ'd;
Asham'd and Angry to be undeceiv'd!
But now LOVE calls me forth; and scarce allows
A moment to the Gods to pay my Vows:
He all Devotion has in disesteem,
But that which we too fondly render him:
LOVE drest me for the day; and both repair,
With an impatient hast to Little Care;
Where many days m' advantage I pursu'd,
But Night returns me to Inquietude;
There suffer'd all that absent Lovers griev'd,
And only knew by what I felt I liv'd;
A thousand little Fears afflict my Heart,
And all its former order quite subvert;
The Beauty's which all day my hope imploy'd,
Seem now too excellent to be enjoy'd.
I number all my RIVALS over now,
Then Raving Mad with Jealousie I grow,
Which does my Flame to that vast height increase;
That here I found, I lov'd to an Excess:

These wild Distractions every Night increase,
But day still reconciles me into Peace;
And I forget amidst their soft Delights,
The unimagin'd torment of the Nights.
'Twas thus a while I liv'd at Little Care,
Without advance of Favour or of fear,
When fair Aminta from that Court departs,
And all her Lovers leave with broken Hearts,
On me alone she does the Grace confer,
In a Permission I shou'd wait on her.
Oh with what eager Joy I did obey!
Joy, which for fear it shou'd my Flame betray,
I Veil'd with Complisance; which Lovers Eyes
Might find transported through the feign'd disguise;
But hers were unconcern'd; or wou'd not see,
The Trophies of their new gain'd Victory:
Aminta now to Good Reception goes;
A place which more of Entertainment shows
Then State or Greatness; where th'Inhabitants,
Are Civil to the height of Complisance;
They Treat all Persons with a chearful Grace,
And show 'em all the pleasures of the Place;
By whose Example bright Aminta too,
Confirm'd her self, and more obliging grew.
Her Smiles and Air more Gracious now appear;
And her Victorious Eyes more sweetness wear:
The wonderous Majesty that drest her Brow,
Becomes less Awful, but more Charming now:
Her Pride abating does my Courage warm,
And promises success from every Charm.
She now permits my Eyes, with timorous Fears,
To tell her of the Wounds she'as made by hers,
Against her Will my Sighs she does approve,
And seems well pleas'd to think they come from Love.
Nothing oppos'd it self to my delight,
But absence from Aminta every Night.
But LOVE, who recompences when he please,
And has for every Cruelty an ease;
Who like to bounteous Heaven, assigns a share
Of future Bliss to those that suffer here:
Led me to HOPE! A City fair and large,
Built with much Beauty, and Adorn'd with Charge.

HOPE.

'Tis wonderous Populous from the excess,
Of Persons from all parts that thither press:

One side of this magnifick City stands,
On a foundation of unfaithful Sands;
Which oftentimes the glorious Load destroys,
Which long designing was with Pomp and Noise;
The other Parts well founded neat and strong,
Less Beautiful, less Business, and less Throng.
'Tis built upon a Rivers Bank, who's clear
And Murmuring Glide delights the Eye and Ear.

The River of PRETENSION.

This River's call'd Pretension; and its source
T' a bordering Mountain owes, from whence with force,
It spreads into the Arms of that calm space,
Where the proud City dayly sees her face;
'Tis treacherously smooth and falsly fair,
Inviting, but undoing to come near;
'Gainst which the Houses there find no defence,
But suffer undermining Violence;
Who while they stand, no Palaces do seem
In all their Glorious Pomp to equal them.

This River's Famous for the fatal Wrecks,
Of Persons most Illustrious of both Sex,
Who to her Bosom with soft Whispers drew,
Then basely smil'd to see their Ruin too.
'Tis there so many Monarchs perisht have,
And seeking Fame alone have found a Grave.
'Twas thither I was tempted too, and LOVE
Maliciously wou'd needs my Conduct prove;
Which Passion now to such a pass had brought,
It gave admittance to the weakest thought,
And with a full carreer to this false Bay
I ran. But met Precaution in my way.
With whom Respect was, who thus gravely said,
Pretension is a River you must Dread:
Fond Youth, decline thy fatal Resolution,
Here unavoidably thou meets Confusion;
Thou fly'st with too much hast to certain Fate,
Follow my Counsel, and be Fortunate.

Asham'd, all Blushing I decline my Eyes,
Yet Bow'd and Thank'd Respect for his advice.
From the bewitching River straight I hy'd,
And hurried to the Cities farthest side
Where lives the Mighty Princess Hope, to whom
The whole Isle as their ORACLE do come;

Tho' little Truth remains in what she says,
Yet all adore her Voice, and her Wise Conduct praise.

The Princess HOPE.

I.
She blows the Youthful Lovers flame,
And promises a sure repose;
Whilst with a Treason void of shame,
His fancy'd Happiness o're-throws.
Her Language is all soft and fair
But her hid Sense is naught but Air,
And can no solid reason bear;
As often as she speaks,
Her faithless Word she breaks;
Great in Pretension, in Performance small,
And when she Swears 'tis Perjury all.
Her Promises like those of Princes are,
Made in Necessity and War,
Cancell'd without remorse, at ease,
In the voluptuous time of Peace.

II.
These are her qualities; but yet
She has a Person full of Charms,
Her Smiles are able to beget
Forgiveness for her other harms;
She's most divinely shap'd, her Eyes are sweet,
And every Glance to please she does employ,
With such address she does all persons treat
As none are weary of her flattery,
She still consoles the most afflicted Hearts,
And makes the Proud vain of his fancy'd Arts.

Amongst the rest of those who dayly came,
T' admire this Princess, and oblige their flame,
(Conducted thither by a false report,
That Happiness resided in her Court)
Two young successless Lovers did resort:
One, so above his Aim had made pretence,
That even to Hope, for him, was Impudence;
Yet he 'gainst Reasons Arguments makes War,
And vainly Swore, his Love did merit her.
Boldly Attempted, daringly Addrest,
And with unblushing Confidence his flame confest.
The other was a Bashful Youth, who made
His Passion his Devotion, not his Trade;

No fond opiniater, who a price
Sets on his Titles, Equipage, or Eyes,
But one that had a thousand Charms in store,
Yet did not understand his Conquering Pow'r:
This Princess with a kind Address receives
These Strangers; and to both new Courage gives.
She animates the haughty to go on!
Says—A Town long besieg'd must needs be won.
Time and Respect remove all obstacles,
And obstinate Love arrives at Miracles.
Were she the Heir to an illustrious Crown,
Those Charms, that haughty meen, that fam'd renown,
That wond'rous skill you do in Verse profess,
That great disdain of common Mistresses;
Can when you please with aid of Billet Deux,
The Royal Virgin to your Arms subdue,
One skill'd in all the Arts to please the fair,
Shou'd be above the Sense of dull despair:
Go on, young noble Warrier, then go on,
Though all the fair are by that Love undone.
Then turning to the other: Sir, said she,
Were the bright Beauty you Adore like me,
Your silent awful Passion more wou'd move,
Than all the bold and forward Arts of Love.
A Heart the softest composition forms,
And sooner yields by treaty, then by storms;
A Look, a Sigh, a Tear, is understood,
And makes more warm disorders in the Blood,
Has more ingaging tender Eloquence,
Then all the industry of Artful Sense:
So falling drops with their soft force alone
Insinuate kind impressions in obdurate stone.
But that which most my pity did imploy,
Was a young Hero, full of Smiles and Joy.
A noble Youth to whom indulgent Heaven,
Had more of Glory then of Virtue given;
Conducted thither by a Politick throng,
The Rabble Shouting as he past along.
Whilst he, vain with the beastly Din they make,
(Which were the same, if Bears were going to stake)
Addresses to this faithless Flatterer;
Who in return, calls him, young God of War!
The Cities Champion! and his Countries Hope,
The Peoples Darling, and Religious Prop.
Scepters and Crowns does to his view expose;
And all the Fancied pow'r of Empire shows.
In vain the Vision he wou'd dis-believe,
In spight of Sense she does his Soul deceive:

He Credits all! nor ask's which way or how,
The dazling Circle shall surround his Brow;
Implicitly attends the flattering Song,
Gives her his easy Faith, and is undone.
For with one turn of State the Frenzy's heal'd,
The Blind recover and the Cheats reveal'd.
Whilst all his Charms of Youth and Beauty lies,
The kind reproach of pitying Enemies.
To me she said, and smiling as she spoke,
Lisander, you with Love have Reason took,
Continue so, and from Aminta's Heart
Expect what Love and Beauty can impart.
I knew she flatter'd, yet I cou'd not choose
But please my Self, and credit the Abuse;
Her charming Words that Night repos'd me more,
Then all the grateful Dreams I'd had before.
Next day I rose, and early with the Sun;
Love guided me to Declaration,
A pleasant City built with Artful Care,
To which the Lovers of the Isle repair.
In our pursuit Respect dissatisfy'd,
Did the unreasonable Adventure chide;
Return, unheedy Youth, cry'd he, return!
Let my advice th' approaching danger warn:
Renounce thy Purpose and thy haste decline,
Or thou wilt ruine all Loves great design;
Amaz'd I stood, and unresolv'd t' obey,
Cou'd not return, durst not pursue my way;
Whilst LOVE, who thought himself concern'd as Guide
I'th' Criminal Adventure, thus reply'd:

LOVE's Resentment.

Must we eternal Martyrdom pursue?
Must we still Love, and always suffer too?
Must we continue still to dye,
And ne'r declare the cruel Cause;
Whilst the fair Murdress asks not why,
But triumphs in her rigorous Laws;
And grows more mighty in disdain,
More Peevish, Humorous, Proud and Vain
The more we languish by our Pain?
And when we Vow, Implore, and Pray,
Shall the Inhumane cruel fair
Only with nice disdain the sufferer pay?
Consult her Pride alone in the affair,
And coldly cry—In time perhaps I may—

Consider and redress the Youth's despair;
And when she wou'd a Period put to's Fate,
Alas, her cruel Mercy comes too late!
But wise Respect obligingly reply'd,
Amintas Cruelty you need not dread,
Your Passion by your Eyes will soon be known,
Without this hast to Declaration;
'Tis I will guide you where you still shall find,
Aminta in best Humour and most kind.

Strong were his Arguments; his Reasonings prove
Too pow'rful for the angry God of Love.
Who by degrees t' his native softness came,
Yields to Respect and owns his haste a blame.
Both vow obedience to his judging Wit,
And to his graver Conduct both submit,
Who now invites us to a Reverend place,
An ancient Town, whose Governor he was.
Impregnable, with Bastions fortify'd,
Guarded with fair built Walls on every side,
The top of which the Eye cou'd scarce discern,
So strong as well secur'd the Rich concern;
Silence with Modesty and Secrecy,
Have all committed to their Custody.
Silence to every questions ask'd, replies
With apt Grimasses of the Face and Eyes;
Her Finger on her Mouth; and as you've seen,
Her Picture, Handsom, with fantastick mean,
Her every Motion her Commands express,
But seldom any the hid Soul confess.
The Virgin Modesty is wond'rous fair,
A bashful Motion, and a blushing Air;
With unassur'd regard her Eyes do move,
Untaught by affectation or Self-love;
Her Robes not gaudy were, nor loosely ty'd,
But even concealing more then need be hid.
For Secrecie, one rarely sees her Face,
Whose lone Apartment is some Dark recess;
From whence unless some great affairs oblige,
She finds it difficult to dis-ingage;
Her voice is low, but subtilly quick her Ears,
And answers still by signs to what she hears.
—Led by Respect we did an entrance get,
Not saying any thing, who ere we met.

The City of DISCRETION.

The Houses there, retir'd in Gardens are,
And all is done with little noise,
One seldom sees Assemblies there,
Or publick shows for Grief or Joys.
One rarely walks but in the Night,
And most endeavour to avoid the Light.
There the whole World their bus'ness carry,
Without or confident, or Secretary:
One still is under great constraint,
Must always suffer, but ne'r make complaint,
'Tis there the dumb and silent languishes,
Are predic'd, which so well explain the Heart:
Which without speaking can so much express,
And secrets to the Soul the nearest way impart;
Language which prettify perswades belief;
Who's silent Eloquence obliges Joy or Grief.

This City's called Discretion, being the name
Of her that is Lieutenant of the same,
And Sister to Respect; a Lady who
Seldom obtains a Conquest at first view;
But in repeated Visits one shall find,
Sufficient Charms of Beauty and of Mind:
Her vigorous piercing Eyes can when they please,
Make themselves lov'd, and understood with Ease.
Not too severe, but yet reserv'd and wise,
And her Address is full of subtilties;
Which upon all occasions serves her turn;
T' express her Kindness, and to hide her scorn;
Dissimulations Arts, she useful holds,
And in good manners sets 'en down for rules.
'Twas here Aminta liv'd, and here I paid
My constant visits to the lovely Maid.
With mighty force upon my Soul I strove,
To hide the Sent'ments of my raging Love.
All that I spoke did but indifferent seem,
Or went no higher than a great esteem.
But 'twas not long my Passion I conceal'd,
My flame in spight of me, it self reveal'd.

The Silent Confession.

And tho' I do not speak, alas,
My Eyes, and Sighs too much do say!
And pale and languishing my Face,
The torments of my Soul betray;
They the sad story do unfold,

Love cannot his own secrets hold;
And though Fear ty's my Tongue, Respect my Eyes,
Yet something will disclose the pain;
Which breaking out throw's all disguise;
Reproaches her with Cruelties;
Which she augments by new disdain;
—Where e're she be, I still am there;
What-ere she do, I that prefer;
In spight of all my strength, at her approach,
I tremble with a sight or touch;
Paleness or Blushes does my Face surprize,
If mine by chance meet her encountering Eyes;
'Twas thus she learn'd my Weakness, and her Pow'r;
And knew too well she was my Conqueror.

And now—
Her Eyes no more their wonted Smiles afford,
But grew more fierce, the more they were ador'd;
The marks of her esteem which heretofore
Rais'd my aspiring flame, oblige no more;
She calls up all her Pride to her defence;
And as a Crime condemns my just pretence;
Me from her presence does in Fury chase;
No supplications can my doom reverse;
And vainly certain of her Victory,
Retir'd into the Den of Cruelty.

The Den of Cruelty.

A Den where Tygers make the passage good,
And all attempting Lovers make their Food;
I'th' hollow of a mighty Rock 'tis plac'd,
Which by the angry Sea is still imbrac'd:
Whose frightful surface constant Tempest wears,
Which strikes the bold Adventurers with Fears.
The Elements their rudest Winds send out,
Which blow continual coldness round about.
Upon the Rock eternal Winter dwells,
Which weeps away in dropping Isicles;
The barren hardness meets no fruitful Ray,
Nor bears it Issue to the God of day;
All bleek and cale, th' unshady prospect lies,
And nothing grateful meets the melancholy Eyes.

To this dire place Aminta goes, whilst I,
Begg'd her with Prayers and Tears to pass it by;
All dying on the Ground my self I cast,

And with my Arms her flying Feet imbrac'd;
But she from the kind force with Fury flung,
And on an old deformed Woman hung.
A Woman frightful, with a horrid Frown,
And o're her angry Eyes, her Brows hung down:
One single Look of hers, fails not t' impart,
A terror and despair to every Heart:
She fills the Universe with discontents,
And Torments for poor Lovers still invents.
This is the mighty Tyrant Cruelty,
Who with the God of Love is still at enmity;
She keeps a glorious Train, and Glorious Court,
And thither Youth and Beauty still resort:
But oh my Soul form'd for Loves softer Sport,
Cou'd not endure the Rigor of her Court!
Which her first rude Address did so affright,
That I all Trembling hasted from her Sight,
Leaving the unconcern'd and cruel Maid,
And on a Rivers Bank my self all fainting laid;
Which River from the obdurate Rock proceeds,
And cast's it self i'th' Melancholy Meads.

The River of Despair.

Its Torrent has no other source,
But Tears from dying Lovers Eyes;
Which mixt with Sighs precipitates its course;
Softning the senseless Rocks in gliding by;
Whose doleful Murmurs have such Eloquence
That even the neighbouring Trees and flow'rs have pitying sense;
And Cruelty alone knows in what sort,
Against the moving sound to make defence,
Who laughs at all despair and Death as sport.

A dismal Wood the Rivers Banks do bear,
Securing even the day from entering there;
The Suns bright Rays a passage cannot find,
Whose Boughs make constant War against the Wind;
Yet through their Leaves glimmers a sullen Light;
Which renders all below more terrible than Night,
And shows upon the Bark of every Tree,
Sad stories carv'd of Love and Cruelty;
The Grove is fill'd with Sighs, with Crys, and Groans,
Reproaches and Complaints in dying Moans;
The Neighbouring Eccho's nothing do repeat,
But what the Soul sends forth with sad regret;
And all things there no other Murmurs make,

But what from Language full of death they take,
'Twas in this place dispairing ere to free
Aminta from the Arms of Cruelty,
That I design'd to render up my Breath,
And charge the cruel Charmer with my Death.

The RESOLVE.

Now, my fair Tyrant, I despise your Pow'r;
'Tis Death, not you becomes my Conqueror;
This easy Trophy which your scorn
Led bleeding by your Chariot-side,
Your haughty Victory to adorn,
Has broke the Fetters of your Pride,
Death takes his quarrel now in hand,
And laughs at all your Eyes can do;
His pow'r thy Beauty can withstand,
Not all your Smiles can the grim victor bow.
He'll hold no Parley with your Wit,
Nor understands your wanton play,
Not all your Arts can force him to submit,
Not all your Charms can teach him to obey;
Your youth nor Beauty can inspire,
His frozen Heart with Love's perswasive fire;
Alas, you cannot warm him to one soft desire;
Oh mighty Death that art above,
The pow'r of Beauty or of Love!

Thus sullen with my Fate sometimes I grew,
And then a fit of softness wou'd ensue,
Then weep, and on my Knees implore my Fair,
And speak as if Aminta present were.

The QUESTION.

Say, my fair Charmer, must I fall,
A Victim to your Cruelty?
And must I suffer as a Criminal?
Is it to Love offence enough to dye?
Is this the recompence at last,
Of all the restless hours I've past?
How oft my Awe, and my Respect,
Have fed your Pride and Scorn?
How have I suffered your neglect,
Too mighty to be born?
How have I strove to hide that flame

You seem'd to disapprove?
How careful to avoid the name
Of Tenderness or Love?
Least at that Word some guilty Blush shou'd own,
What your bright Eyes forbad me to make known.

Thus fill'd the neighbouring Eccho's with my Cry,
Did nothing but reproach, complain and dye:
One day—
All hopeless on the Rivers Brink I stood,
Resolv'd to plunge into the Rapid Floud,
That Floud that eases Lovers in despair,
And puts an end to all their raging care:
'Tis hither those betray'd by Beauty come,
And from this kinder stream receive their doom;
Here Birds of Ominous presages Nest,
Securing the forlorn Inhabitants from rest:
Here Mid-night-Owls, night-Crows, and Ravens dwell,
Filling the Air with Melancholy Yell:
Here swims a thousand Swans, whose doleful moan
Sing dying Loves Requiems with their own:
I gaz'd around, and many Lovers view'd,
Gastly and pale, who my design pursu'd;
But most inspir'd by some new hope, or won
To finish something they had left undone;
Some grand Important bus'ness of their Love,
Did from the fatal precipice remove:
For me, no Reason my designs disswade,
Till Love all Breathless hasted to my Aid;
With force m' unfixing Feet he kindly graspt,
And tenderly reproacht my desperate hast,
Reproach'd my Courage, and condemn'd my Wit,
That meanly cou'd t' a Womans scorn submit,
That cou'd to feed her Pride, and make her vain,
Destroy an Age of Life, for a short date of pain:
He wou'd have left me here, but that I made,
So many friendships as did soon perswade
The yielding Boy, who Smil'd, resolv'd and staid.
He rais'd my Head, and did again renew,
His Flatteries, and all the Arts he knew:
To call my Courage to its wonted place.
What, cry'd he—(sweetly Angry) shall a Face
Arm'd with the weak resistance of a Frown,
Force us to lay our Claims and Titles down?
Shall Cruelty a peevish Woman prove,
Too strong to be overcome by Youth and Love?
No! rally all thy Vigor, all thy Charms,
And force her from the cruel Tyrants Arms;

Come, once more try th' incens'd Maid to appease,
Death's in our pow'r to grasp when ere we please;
He said—And I the heavenly voice attend,
Whilst towards the Rock our hasty steps we bend,
Before the Gates with all our forces lye,
Resolv'd to Conquer, or resolv'd to dye;
In vain Love all his feeble Engines rears,
His soft Artillery of Sighs and Tears,
Were all in vain—against the Winds were sent,
For she was proof 'gainst them and Languishment:
Repeated Vows and Prayers mov'd no Remorse,
And 'twas to Death alone I had Recourse:
Love in my Anguish bore a mighty part,
He pityed, but he cou'd not ease my Heart:
A thousand several ways he had assay'd,
To touch the Heart of this obdurate Maid;
Rebated all his Arrow's still return,
For she was fortify'd with Pride and Scorn.
The useless Weapons now away he flung,
Neglected lay his Ivory Bow unstrung,
His gentle Azure Wings were all unprun'd,
And the gay Plumes a fading Tinct assum'd;
Which down his snowy sides extended lay,
And now no more in wanton Motions play.
He blusht to think he had not left one dart,
Of force enough to wound Aminta's Heart;
He blusht to think she shou'd her freedom boast,
Whilst mine from the first Dart he sent was lost:
Thus tir'd with our Complaints; (whilst no relief
Rescu'd the fleeting Soul from killing Grief)
We saw a Maid approach, who's lovely Face
Disdain'd the Beauties of the common race:
Soft were her Eyes, where unfeign'd Sorrow dwelt,
And on her Cheeks in pitying Show'rs they melt:
Soft was her Voice, and tenderly it strook,
The eager listening Soul, when e're she spoke;
And what did yet my Courage more augment,
She wore this sadness for my languishment.

And sighing said, ah Gods! have you
Beheld this dying Youth, and never found
A pity for a Heart so true,
Which dyes adoring her that gave the Wound?
His Youth, his Passion, and his Constancy,
Merits, ye God's, a kinder Destiny.

With pleasure I attended what she said,
And wonder'd at the friendship of the Maid.

Of LOVE I ask'd her name? who answer'd me,
'Twas Pity: Enemy to Cruelty:
Who often came endeavouring to abate,
The Languishments of the unfortunate;
And said, if she wou'd take my injur'd part,
She soon wou'd soften fair Aminta's Heart;
For she knows all the subtillest Arts to move,
And teach the timorous Virgin how to love.
With Joy I heard, and my Address apply'd,
To gain the Beauteous Pity to my Side:
Nothing I left untold that might perswade,
The listening Virgin to afford her aid.
Told her my Passions, Sorrows, Pains and Fears,
And whilst I spoke, confirm'd 'em with my Tears;
All which with down-cast Eyes she did attend,
And blushing said, my Tale had made a Friend;
I bow'd and thankt her with a chearful look,
Which being return'd by hers, her leave she took:
Now to Aminta all in haste she hyes,
Whom she assail'd with sorrow in her Eyes,
And a sad story of my Miseries,
Which she with so much tenderness exprest,
As forc'd some Sighs from the fair Charmers Breast;
The subtil Pity found she should prevail,
And oft repeats th' insinuating Tale,
And does insensibly the Maid betray,
Where Love and I, Panting and Trembling lay;
Where she beheld th' effects of her disdain,
And in my languid Face she read my Pain.
Down her fair Cheeks some pitying drops did glide;
Which cou'd not be restrain'd by feebler Pride;
Against my anguish she had no defence,
Such Charms had grief, my Tears such Eloquence;
My Sighs and Murmurs she began t' approve,
And listen'd to the story of my LOVE.
With tenderness, she did my Sufferings hear,
And even my Reproaches now cou'd bear:
At last my trembling Hand in hers she took,
And with a charming Blush, these Words she spoke:

I.
Faithful Lisander, I your Vows approve,
And can no longer hide.
My Sense of all your suffering Love,
With the thin Veil of Pride.

II.
'Twas long in Vain that Pity did assail,

My cold and stubborn Heart;
Ere on th' insensible she cou'd prevail,
To render any Part.

III.
To her for all the tenderness,
Which in my Eyes you find,
You must your gratitude express,
'Tis Pity only makes me kind.

IV.
Live then, Lisander, since I must confess,
In spight of all my native modesty,
I cannot wish that you shou'd Love me less;
Live then and hope the Circling Sun may see
In his swift course a grateful change in me,
And that in time your Passion may receive
All you dare take, and all a Maid may give.

Oh, Lysidas, I cannot here relate,
The Sense of Joy she did in me create;
The sudden Blessing overcame me so,
It almost finisht, what Grief fail'd to do;
I wanted Courage for the soft surprize,
And waited re-enforcements from her Eyes:
At last with Transports which I cou'd not hide,
Raising my self from off the ground, I cry'd.

The TRANSPORT.

Rejoyce! my new made happy Soul, Rejoyce!
Bless the dear minute, bless the Heav'nly voice,
That has revok't thy fatal doom;
Rejoyce! Aminta leads thee from the Tomb.
Banish the anxious thoughts of dying hours,
Forget the shades and melancholy Bow'rs,
Thy Eyes so oft bedew'd with falling show'rs;
Banish all Thoughts that do remain,
Of Sighing Days and Nights of Pain,
When on neglected Beds of Moss thou'st lain:
Oh happy Youth! Aminta bids thee live;
Thank not the sullen God's or defer Stars,
Since from her Hand thou dost the Prize receive;
Hers be the Service, as the bounty hers;
For all that Life must dedicated be,
To the fair God-like Maid that gave it Thee.

Now, Lysidas, behold my happy State;
Behold me Blest, behold me Fortunate,
And from the height of languishing despair,
Rais'd to the Glory of Aminta's care:
And this one moment of my Heaven of Joy,
Did the remembrance of past Griefs destroy:
And Pity ceas'd not here; but with new Eloquence,
Obliges the shy Maid to visit Confidence.

CONFIDENCE.

A Lady lovely, with a charming Meen,
Gay, frank, and open, and an Air serene;
In every Look she does her Soul impart,
With ease one reads the Sent'ments of her Heart;
Her Humour generous, and her Language free,
And all her Conversation graceful Liberty:
Her Villa is Youth's general Rendezvous,
Where in delightful Gardens, winding Groves,
The happy Lovers dwell with secresie,
Un-interrupted by fond Jealousie:
'Tis there with Innocence, they do and say
A thousand things, to pass the short-liv'd day:
There free from censuring Spies, they entertain,
And pleasures tast, un-intermixt with pain.

'Tis there we see, what most we do adore,
And yet we languish to discover more.
Hard fate of Lovers, who are ne'er content,
In an Estate so Blest and Innocent.
But still press forward, urg'd by soft desires,
To Joys that oft extinguishes their Fires;
In this degree I found a happiness,
Which nought but wishing more cou'd render less.
I saw Aminta here without controul,
And told her all the Secrets of my Soul;
Whilst she t' express her height of Amity,
Communicated all her Thoughts to me.

The REFLECTION.

Oh with what Pleasure did I pass away.
The too swift course of the delightful day!
What Joys I found in being a Slave
To every Conquering Smile she gave,
Whose every sweetness wou'd inspire

The Cinick and the Fool with Love;
Alas, I needed no more Fire,
Who did its height already prove:
Ah my Aminta! had I been content,
With this degree of Ravishment,
With the nee'r satisfy'd delight I took,
Only to prattle Love, to sigh and look,
With the dull Bartering Kiss for Kiss,
And never aim'd at higher Bliss,
With all the stealths forgetful Lovers make,
When they their Little Covenants break:
To these sad shades of Death I'd not been hurl'd,
And thou mightst still have blest the drooping World;
But though my Pleasure were thus vast and high,
Yet Loves insatiate Luxury
Still wish'd reveal'd the unknown Mystery.

But still Love importun'd, nor cou'd I rest,
So often, and impatiently he prest,
That I the lovely Virgin wou'd invite,
To the so worshipp'd Temple of Delight.
By all the Lovers Arts I strove to move,
And watch the softest Minutes of her Love,
Which against all my Vows and Prayers were proof.
Alas she lov'd, but did not love enough:
And I cou'd no returns but Anger get,
Her Heart was not intirely conquer'd yet;
For liking, I mistook her Complysance,
And that for Love; when 'twas her Confidence.
But 'twas not long my Sighs I did imploy,
Before she rais'd me to the height of Joy.
And all my Fears and Torments to remove,
Yields I shall lead her to the Court of LOVE.
Here, Lysidas, thou thinks me sure and blest,
With Recompence for all my past unrest;
But fortun'd smil'd the easier to betray,
She's less inconstant than a Lover's Joy:
For whilst our Chariot Wheels out-stript the Wind,
Leaving all thought of Mortal Cares behind,
Whilst we sate gazing full of new surprize,
Exchanging Souls from eithers darting Eyes,
We encounter'd One who seem'd of great Command,
Who seiz'd the Reins with an all-pow'rful hand:
Awful his looks, but rude in his Address,
And his Authority roughly did express;
His violent Hands he on Aminta laid,
And out of mine snatch'd the dear trembling Maid;
So suddenly as hinder'd my defence,

And she cou'd only say in parting thence,
Forgive, Lisander, what by force I do,
Since nothing else can ravish me from you;
Make no resistance, I obey [A]Devoir.
Who values not thy Tears, thy Force or Prayer,
Retain thy Faith and Love Aminta still,
Since she abandons thee against her Will.
Immoveable I remain'd with this surprize,
Nor durst reply so much as with my Eyes.
I saw her go, but was of Sense bereav'd,
And only knew from what I heard, I liv'd;
Yes, yes, I heard her last Commands, and thence
By violent degrees retriev'd my Sense.
Ye Gods, in this your Mercy was severe,
You might have spar'd the useless favour here.
But the first Thoughts my Reason did conceive,
Were to pursue the injurious Fugitive.
Raving, that way I did my haste direct,
But once more met the Reverend Respect,
From whom I strove my self to dis-ingage,
And faign'd a calmness to disguise my Rage.
In vain was all the Cheat, he soon perceiv'd,
Spight of my Smiles, how much, and why I griev'd;
Saw my despairs, and what I meant to do,
And begg'd I wou'd the rash Design forego;
A thousand dangers he did represent,
T' win me from the desperate attempt.
I ever found his Counsel just and good,
And now resolv'd it shou'd not be withstood;
Thus he ore-came my Rage, but did not free,
My Soul from Griefs more painful Tyranny;
Grief tho' more soft, did not less cruel prove,
Madness is easier far then hopeless Love.
I parted thus, but knew not what to do;
Nor where I went; nor did I care to know;
With folded Arms, with weeping Eyes declin'd,
I search the unknown shade, I cou'd not find,
And mixt my constant Sighs with flying Wind.
By slow unsteady steps the Paths I trace,
Which undesign'd conduct me to a place
Fit for a Soul distrest; obscur'd with shade,
Lonely and fit for Love and Sorrow made;
The Murmuring Boughs themselves together twist,
And 'twou'd allow to Grief her self some rest.
Inviron'd 'tis with lofty Mountains round,
From whence the Eccho's, Sighs, and Crys rebound;
Here in the midst and thickest of the Wood,
Cover'd with bending Shades a Castle stood,

Where Absence that dejected Maid remains,
Who nothing but her Sorrow entertains.

[A] Duty.

ABSENCE.

Her mourning languid Eyes are rarely shown,
Unless to those afflicted like her own;
Her lone Apartment all obscure as Night,
Discover'd only by a glimmering Light:
Weeping she sate, her Face with Grief dismaid,
Which all its natural sweetness has decaid;
Yet in despight of Grief there does appear,
The ruin'd Monuments of what was fair,
E'r cruel Love and Grief had took possession there.
These made her old without the aid of Years;
Worn out, and faint with lingring hopes and fears,
She seldom answers ought but with her Tears.
No Train attends, she only is obey'd
By Melancholy, that soft, silent Maid:
A Maid that fits her Humour every way,
With whom she passes all the tedious day:
No other object can her Mind content,
She Feeds and Flatters all her languishment;
The noisy Streams that from high Mountains fall;
And water all the Neighbouring flowry Vale:
The Murmurs of the Rivulets that glide,
Against the bending Seges on the side;
Of mournful Birds the sad and tuneful Noats,
The Bleats of straggling Lambs, and new yean'd Goats:
The distant Pipe of some lone Mountain Swain,
Who to his injur'd Passion fits his strain;
Is all the Harmony her Soul can entertain.

On a strict league of Friendship we agree,
For I was sad, and as forlorn as she;
To all her Humours, I conform my own,
Together Sigh, together Weep, and Moan;
Like her to Woods and Fountains I retreat,
And urge the pitying Eccho's to repeat
My tale of Love, and at each Period found
Aminta's name, and bear it all around,
Whilst listening Voices do the charm reply,
And lost in mixing Air, together dye.
There minutes like dull days creep slowly on,
And every day I drag an Age along;

The coming hours cou'd no more pleasures hast,
Than those so insupportably I'd past.
I rav'd, I wept, I wisht, but all in vain,
The distant Maid, nor saw, nor eas'd my pain;
With my sad tale, each tender Bark I fill,
This—soft complaints, and that—my Ravings tell;
This bears vain Curses on my cruel fate,
And Blessings on the Charming Virgin, that;
The Willow by the lonely Spring that grows,
And o're the Stream bends his forsaken Boughs,
I call Lisander; they, like him, I find,
Murmur and ruffl'd are with every Wind.
On the young springing Beech that's straight and tall,
I Carve her name, and that Aminta call;
But where I see an Oak that Climbs above
The rest, and grows the Monster of the Grove;
Whose pow'rful Arms when aiding Winds do blow,
Dash all the tender twining Shades below,
And even in Calms maliciously do spread,
That naught beneath can thrive, imbrace or breed;
Whose mischiefs far exceed his fancy'd good,
Honour I call him: Tyrant of the Wood.
Thus rove from Thought to Thought without relief:
A change 'tis true; but 'tis from Grief to Grief;
Which when above my silence they prevail,
With Love I'm froward, on my Fortune rail,
And to the Winds breathe my neglected Tale.

To LOVE.

I.

Fond Love thy pretty Flatteries cease,
That feeble Hope you give;
Unless 'twould make my happiness,
In vain, dear Boy; in vain you strive,
It cannot keep my tortur'd Heart alive.

II.

Tho' thou shou'dst give me all the Joys,
Luxurious Monarch's do possess,
Without Aminta 'tis but empty noise,
Dull and insipid happiness;
And you in vain invite me to a Feast,
Where my Aminta cannot be a Guest.

III.

Ye glorious Trifles, I renounce ye all,

Since she no part of all your splendour makes;
Let the Dull unconcern'd obey your call,
Let the gay Fop, who his Pert Courtship takes;
For Love, whilst he profanes your Deity,
Be Charm'd and Pleas'd with all your necessary vanity.

IV.
But give me leave, whose Soul's inspir'd,
With sacred, but desparing Love.
To dye from all your noise retir'd,
And Buried lie within this silent Grove.
For whilst I Live, my Soul's a prey,
To insignificant desires,
Whilst thou fond God of Love and Play,
With all thy Darts, with all thy useless Fires,
With all thy wanton flatteries cannot charm,
Nor yet the frozen-hearted Virgin warm.

V.
Others by absence Cure their fire,
Me it inrages more with pain;
Each thought of my Aminta blows it higher,
And distance strengthens my desire;
I Faint with wishing, since I wish in vain;
Either be gone, fond Love, or let me dye,
Hopeless desire admits no other remedy.

Here 'twas the height of Cruelty I prov'd,
By absence from the sacred Maid I lov'd:
And here had dy'd, but that Love found a way,
Some letters from Aminta to convey,
Which all the tender marks of pity gave,
And hope enough to make me wish to Live.
From Duty, now the lovely Maid is freed,
And calls me from my lonely solitude:
Whose cruel Memory in a Moments space,
The thoughts of coming Pleasures quite deface;
With an impatent Lovers hast I flew,
To the vast Blessing Love had set in view,
But oh I found Aminta in a place,
Where never any Lover happy was!

RIVALS.

Rivals 'tis call'd, a Village where,
The Inhabitants in Fury still appear;
Malicious paleness, or a generous red,

O'r every angry face is spread,
Their Eyes are either smiling with disdain,
Or fiercely glow with raging Fire.
Gloomy and sullen with dissembl'd pain,
Love in the Heart, Revenge in the desire:
Combates, Duels, Challenges,
Is the discourse, and all the business there.
Respect of Blood, nor sacred friendship tyes;
Can reconcile the Civil War,
Rage, Horror, Death, and wild despair,
Are still Rencounter'd, and still practised there.

'Twas here the lovely cruel Maid I found,
Incompass'd with a thousand Lovers round;
At my approach I saw their Blushes rise,
And they regarded me with angry Eyes.
Aminta too, or else my Fancy 'twas,
Receiv'd me with a shy and cold Address,
—I cou'd not speak—but Sigh'd, retir'd and Bow'd;
With pain I heard her Talk and Laugh aloud,
And deal her Freedoms to the greedy Crowd.
I Curst her Smiles, and envy'd every look,
And Swore it was too kind, what'ere she spoke;
Condemn'd her Air, rail'd on her soft Address,
And vow'd her Eyes did her false Heart confess,
And vainly wisht their Charming Beauties less.
A Secret hatred in my Soul I bear,
Against these objects of my new despair;
I waited all the day, and all in vain;
Not one lone minute snatcht, to ease my pain;
Her Lovers went and came in such a sort,
It rather seem'd Loves-Office than his Court,
Made for eternal Bus'ness, not his Sport,
Love saw my pain, and found my rage grew high,
And led me off, to lodge at Jealousie.

JEALOUSIE.

I.
A Palace that is more uneasy far,
Then those of cruelty and absence are,
There constant show'rs of Hail and Rains do flow,
Continual Murmuring Winds around do blow,
Eternal Thunder rowling in the Air,
And thick dark hanging Clouds the day obscure;
Whose sullen dawn all Objects multiplies.
And render things that are not, to the Eyes.

Fantoms appear by the dull gloomy light,
That with such subtil Art delude the sight,
That one can see no Object true or right.
I here transported and impatient grow
And all things out of order do;
Hasty and peevish every thing I say,
Suspicion and distrust's my Passions sway,
And bend all Nature that uneasy way.

II.
A thousand Serpents gnaw the Heart;
A thousand Visions fill the Eyes,
And Deaf to all that can relief impart,
We hate the Counsel of the Wise,
And Sense like Tales of Lunaticks despise:
Faithless, as Couzen'd Maids, by Men undone,
And obstinate as new Religion,
As full of Error, and false Notion too,
As Dangerous, and as Politick;
As Humerous as a Beauty without Wit;
As Vain and Fancyful in all we do:
—Thus Wreck the Soul, as if it did conceal,
Love Secrets which by torturing 'two'd reveal.

Restless and wild, ranging each Field and Grove;
I meet the Author of my painful Love;
But still surrounded with a numerous Train
Of Lovers, whom Love taught to Sigh and Fawn,
At my approach, my Soul all Trembling flies,
And tells its soft Resentment at my Eyes:
My Face all pale, my steps unsteady fall,
And faint Confusion spreads it self o're all.
I listen to each low breath'd Word she says,
And the returns the happy Answerer pays:
When catching half the Sense, the rest Invent,
And turn it still to what will most Torment;
If any thing by Whispers she impart,
'Tis Mortal, 'tis a Dagger at my Heart;
And every Smile, each Motion, Gesture, Sign,
In favour of some Lover I explain:
When I am absent, in some Rivals Arms,
I Fancy she distributes all her Charms,
And if alone I find her; sighing cry,
Some happier Lover she expects than I.
So that I did not only Jealous grow,
Of all I saw; but all I fancy'd too.

The COMPLAINT.

I.

Oft in my Jealous Transports I wou'd cry,
Ye happy shades, ye happy Bow'rs,
Why speaks she tenderer things to you than me?
Why does she Smile, carress and praise your Flowers?
Why Sighs she (opening Buds) her Secrets all
Into your fragrant Leaves?
Why does she to her Aid your sweetness call,
Yet take less from you than she gives?
Why on your Beds must you be happy made,
And be together with Aminta laid?
You from her Hands and Lips may KISSES take,
And never meet Reproaches from her Pride;
A thousand Ravishing stealths may make,
And even into her softer Bosome glide.
And there expire! Oh happy Rival flowers,
How vainly do I wish my Fate like that of Yours?

II.

Tell me, ye silent Groves, whose Gloom invites,
The lovely Charmer to your Solitudes?
Tell me for whom she languishes and sighs?
For whom she feels her soft Inquietudes?
Name me the Youth for whom she makes her Vows,
For she has breath'd it oft amongst your listening Boughs?
Oh happy confidents of her Amours,
How vainly do I wish my Fortune blest as Yours.

III.

Oh happy Brooks, oh happy Rivulets,
And Springs that in a thousand Windings move;
Upon your Banks how oft Aminta sits,
And prattles to you all her Tale of Love:
Whilst your smooth surface little Circles bears,
From the Impressions of her falling Tears,
And as you wantonly reflecting pass,
Glide o're the lovely Image of her Face;
And sanctifies your stream, which as you run,
You Boast in Murmurs to the Banks along.
Dear Streams! to whom she gives her softest hours,
How vainly do I wish my happiness like yours.

Sometimes I rail'd again, and wou'd upbraid,
Reproachfully, the charming fickle Maid:
Sometimes I vow'd to do't no more,
But one, vain, short-liv'd hour,

Wou'd Perjure all I'd Sworn before,
And Damn my fancy'd Pow'r.
Sometimes the sullen fit wou'd last,
A teadious live-long day:
But when the wrecking hours were past,
With what Impatience wou'd I hast,
And let her Feet weep my neglect away.
Quarrels are the Reserves Love keeps in store,
To aid his Flames and make 'em burn the more.

The PENITENT.

I.

With Rigor Arm your self, (I cry'd)
It is but just and fit;
I merit all this Treatment from your Pride,
All the reproaches of your Wit;
Put on the cruel Tyrant as you will,
But know, my tender Heart adores you still.

II.

And yet that Heart has Murmur'd too,
And been so insolent to let you know,
It did complain, and rave, and rail'd at you;
Yet all the while by every God I swear,
By every pitying Pow'r the wretched hear;
By all those Charms that dis-ingage,
My Soul from the extreams of Rage;
By all the Arts you have to save and kill,
My faithful tender Heart adores you still.

III.

But oh you shou'd excuse my soft complaint,
Even my wild Ravings too prefer,
I sigh, I burn, I weep, I faint,
And vent my Passions to the Air;
Whilst all my Torment, all my Care
Serves but to make you put new Graces on,
You Laugh, and Rally my despair,
Which to my Rivals renders you more fair;
And but the more confirms my being undone:
Sport with my Pain as gayly as you will,
My fond, my tender Heart adores you still.

My differing Passions thus, did never cease,
Till they had touch'd her Soul with tenderness;
My Rivals now are banish'd by degrees,

And with 'em all my Fears and Jealousies;
And all advanc'd, as if design'd to please.

The City of LOVE.

In this vast Isle a famous City stands,
Who for its Beauty all the rest Commands,
Built to delight the wondering Gazers Eyes,
Of all the World the great Metropolis.
Call'd by LOVE's name: and here the Charming God,
When he retires to Pleasure, makes abode;
'Tis here both Art and Nature strive to show,
What Pride, Expence, and Luxury, can do,
To make it Ravishing and Awful too:
All Nations hourly thither do resort,
To add a splendour to this glorious Court;
The Young, the Old, the Witty, and the Wise,
The Fair, the Ugly, Lavish, and Precise;
Cowards and Braves, the Modest, and the Lowd,
Promiscuously are blended in the Crowd.
From distant Shoars young Kings their Courts remove,
To pay their Homage to the God of Love.
Where all their sacred awful Majesty,
Their boasted and their fond Divinity;
Loose their vast force; as lesser Lights are hid,
When the fierce God of Day his Beauties spread.
The wondering World for Gods did Kings adore,
Till LOVE confirm'd 'em Mortal by his Pow'r;
And in Loves Court, do with their Vassals live,
Without or Homage, or Prerogative:
Which the young God, not only Blind must show,
But as Defective in his Judgment too.

LOVE's Temple.

Midst this Gay Court a famous Temple stands,
Old as the Universe which it commands;
For mighty Love a sacred being had,
Whilst yet 'twas Chaos, e're the World was made,
And nothing was compos'd without his Aid.
Agreeing Attoms by his pow'r were hurl'd,
And Love and Harmony compos'd the World.
'Tis rich, 'tis solemn all! Divine yet Gay!
From the Jemm'd Roof the dazling Lights display,
And all below inform without the Aids of day.
All Nations hither bring rich offerings,

And 'tis endow'd with Gifts of Love-sick Kings.
Upon an Altar (whose unbounded store
Has made the Rifled Universe so poor,
Adorn'd with all the Treasure of the Seas,
More than the Sun in his vast course surveys)
Was plac'd the God! with every Beauty form'd,
Of Smiling Youth, but Naked, unadorn'd.
His painted Wings displaid: His Bow laid by,
(For here Love needs not his Artillery)
One of his little Hands aloft he bore,
And grasp'd a wounded Heart that burnt all o're,
Towards which he lookt with lovely Laughing Eyes:
As pleas'd and vain, with the fond Sacrifice,
The other pointing downward seem'd to say,
Here at my Feet your grateful Victims lay,
Whilst in a Golden Tablet o're his Head,
In Diamond Characters this Motto stood,
Behold the Pow'r that Conquers every GOD.
The Temple Gates are open Night and Day,
Love's Votaries at all hours Devotions pay,
A Priest of Hymen gives attendance near,
But very rarely shows his Function here,
For Priest cou'd ne'r the Marriage-cheat improve,
Were there no other Laws, but those of Love!
A Slavery generous Heav'n did ne'r design,
Nor did its first lov'd Race of men confine;
A Trick, that Priest, whom Avarice cunning made,
Did first contrive, then sacred did perswade,
That on their numerous and unlucky Race,
They might their base got Wealth securely place.
Curse—cou'd they not their own loose Race inthral,
But they must spread the infection over all!
That Race, whose Brutal heat was grown so wild,
That even the Sacred Porches they defil'd;
And Ravisht all that for Devotion came,
Their Function, nor the Place restrains their flame.
But Love's soft Votaries no such injuries fear,
No pamper'd Levits are in Pension here;
Here are no fatted Lambs to Sacrifice,
No Oyl, fine Flower, or Wines of mighty price,
The subtil Holy Cheats to Gormandize.
Love's soft Religion knows no Tricks nor Arts,
All the Attoning Offerings here are Hearts.
The Mystery's silent, without noyse or show,
In which the Holy Man has nought to do,
The Lover is both Priest and Victim too.
Hither with little force I did perswade,
My lovely timorously yielding Maid,

Implor'd we might together Sacrifice,
And she agrees with Blushing down-cast Eyes;
'Twas then we both our Hearts an Offering made,
Which at the Feet of the young God we laid,
With equal Flames they Burnt; with equal Joy,
But with a Fire that neither did destroy;
Soft was its Force and Sympathy with them,
Dispers'd it self through every trembling Limb;
We cou'd not hide our tender new surprize,
We languisht and confest it with our Eyes;
Thus gaz'd we—when the Sacrifice perform'd,
We found our Hearts entire—but still they burn,
But by a Blessed change in taking back,
The lovely Virgin did her Heart mistake:
Her Bashful Eyes favour'd Love's great design,
I took her Burning Victim: and she mine.
Thus, Lysidas, without constraint or Art,
I reign'd the Monarch of Aminta's Heart;
My great, my happy Title she allows,
And makes me Lord of all her tender Vows,
All my past Griefs in coming Joys were drown'd,
And with eternal Pleasure I was Crown'd;
My Blessed hours in the extream of Joy,
With my soft Languisher I still imploy;
When I am Gay, Love Revels in her Eyes,
When sad—there the young God all panting lies.
A thousand freedoms now she does impart,
Shows all her tenderness dis-rob'd of Art,
But oh this cou'd not satisfy my Heart.
A thousand Anguishes that still contains,
It sighs, and heaves, and pants with pleasing pains.
We look, and Kiss, and Press with new desire,
Whilst every touch Blows the unusual Fire.
For Love's last Mystery was yet conceal'd,
Which both still languisht for, both wisht reveal'd:
Which I prest on—and faintly she deny'd,
With all the weak efforts of dying Pride,
Which struggled long for Empire in her Soul,
Where it was wont to rule without controul.
But Conquering Love had got possession now,
And open'd every Sally to the Foe:
And to secure my doubting happiness,
Permits me to conduct her to the Bow'r of Bliss.
That Bow'r that does eternal Pleasures yield,
Where Psyche first the God of Love beheld:
But oh, in entering this so blest abode,
All Gay and Pleas'd as a Triumphing God,
I new unlook'd for difficulties meet,

Encount'ring Honour at the sacred Gate.

HONOUR.

I.

Honour's a mighty Phantom! which around
The sacred Bower does still appear;
All Day it haunts the hallow'd ground.
And hinders Lovers entering there.
It rarely ever takes its flight,
But in the secret shades of night.
Silence and gloom the charm can soonest end,
And are the luckyest hours to lay the Fiend,
Then 'tis the Vision only will remove,
With Incantations of soft Vows of Love.

II.

But as a God he's Worshipt here,
By all the lovely, young, and fair,
Who all their kind desires controul,
And plays the Tyrant o're the Soul:
His chiefest Attributes, are Pride and Spight,
His pow'r, is robbing Lovers of delight,
An Enemy to Humane kind,
But most to Youth severe;
As Age ill-natur'd, and as ignorance Blind,
Boasting, and Baffled too, as Cowards are;
Fond in opinion, obstinately Wise,
Fills the whole World with bus'ness and with noise.

III.

Where wert thou born? from what didst thou begin?
And what strange Witchcraft brought thy Maxims in?
What hardy Fool first taught thee to the Crowd?
Or who the Duller Slaves that first believ'd?
Some Woman sure, ill-natur'd, old, and proud,
Too ugly ever to have been deceiv'd;
Unskill'd in Love; in Virtue, or in Truth,
Preach'd thy false Notions first, aud so debaucht our Youth.

IV.

And as in other Sectuaries you find,
His Votaries most consist of Womankind,
Who Throng t' adore the necessary Evil,
But most for fear, as Indians do the Devil.
Peevish, uneasy all; for in Revenge,
Love shoots 'em with a thousand Darts.

They feel, but not confess the change;
Their false Devotion cannot save their Hearts.
Thus while the Idol Honour they obey,
Swift time comes on, and blooming Charms decay,
And Ruin'd Beauty does too late the Cheat betray.

This Goblin here—the lovely Maid Alarms,
And snatch'd her, even from my Trembling Arms,
With all the Pow'r of Non-sence he commands,
Which she for mighty Reason understands.
Aminta, fly, he crys! fly, heedless Maid,
For if thou enter'st this Bewitching shade,
Thy Flame, Content, and Lover, all are lost,
And thou no more of Him, or Fame shall boast,
The charming Pleasure soon the Youth will cloy,
And what thou wouldst preserve, that will destroy.
Oh hardy Maid by too much Love undone,
Where are thy Modesty, and Blushes gone?
Where's all that Virtue made thee so Ador'd?
For Beauty stript of Virtue, grows abhorr'd:
Dyes like a flower whose scent quick Poyson gives,
Though every gawdy Glory paints its leaves;
Oh fly, fond Maid, fly that false happiness,
That will attend Thee in the Bower of Bliss.

Thus spoke the Phantom, while the listening Maid,
Took in the fatal Councel; and obey'd:
Frighted she flys, even from the Temple door,
And left me fainting on the sacred floor:
LOVE saw my Griefs, and to my rescue came,
Where on his Bosom, thus I did complain.

The LOSS.

Weep, weep, Lysander, for the lovely Maid,
To whom thy sacred Vows were paid;
Regardless of thy Love, thy Youth, thy Vows,
The Dull Advice of Honour now pursues;
Oh say my lovely Charmer, where
Is all that softness gone?
Your tender Voice and Eyes did wear,
When first I was undone.
Oh whether are your Sighs and Kisses fled?
Where are those clasping Arms,
That left me oft with Pleasures dead,
With their Excess of Charms?
Where is the Killing Language of thy Tongue,

That did the Ravisht Soul surprize?
Where is that tender Rhetorick gone,
That flow'd so softly in thy Eyes?
That did thy heavenly face so sweetly dress,
That did thy wonderous Soul so well express?
All fled with Honour on a Phantom lost;
Where Youth's vast store must perish unpossest.
Ah, my dear Boy, thy loss with me bemoan,
The lovely Fugitive is with Honour gone!

Love laughing spread his Wings and mounting flies,
As swift as Lightning through the yielding Skies,
Where Honour bore away the Trembling Prize.
There at her Feet the Little Charmer falls,
And to his Aid his powerful softness calls:
Assails her with his Tears, his Sighs and Crys,
Th' unfailing Language of his Tongue and Eyes.

Return, said he, return oh fickle Maid,
Who solid Joys abandon'st for a shade;
urn and behold the Slaughter of thy Eyes;
See—the Heart-broken Youth all dying lyes.
Why dost thou follow this Phantastick spright?
This faithless Ignis Fatuus of the Light?
This Foe to Youth, and Beauties worst Disease,
Tyrant of Wit, of Pleasure, and of Ease;
Of all substantial Harms he Author is,
But never pays us back one solid Bliss.
—You'll urge, your Fame is worth a thousand Joys;
Deluded Maid, trust not to empty noise,
A sound, that for a poor Esteem to gain,
Damns thy whole Life t' uneasyness and pain.
Mistaken Virgin, that which pleases me
I cannot by another tast and see;
And what's the complementing of the World to thee?
No, no, return with me, and there receive,
What poor, what scanted Honour cannot give,
Starve not those Charms that were for pleasure made,
Nor unpossest let the rich Treasure fade.
When time comes on; Honour that empty word,
Will leave thee then fore-slighted Age to guard;
Honour as other faithless Lovers are,
Is only dealing with the young and fair;
Approaching Age makes the false Hero fly,
He's Honour with the Young, but with the old necessity.

—Thus said the God! and all the while he spoke,
Her Heart new Fire, her Eyes new softness took.

Now crys, I yield, I yield the Victory!
Lead on, young Charming Boy, I follow thee;
Lead to Lysander, quickly let's be gone,
I am resolv'd to Love, and be undone;
I must not, cannot, Love at cheaper rate,
Love is the word, Lysander and my fate.

Thus to my Arms Love brought the trembling Maid;
Who on my Bosom sighing, softly, said:
Take, charming Victor—what you must—subdue—
'Tis Love—and not Aminta gives it you,
Love that o're all, and every part does reign,
And I shou'd plead-and struggle—but in vain;
Take what a yielding Virgin—can bestow,
I am—dis-arm'd—of all resistance now.—
Then down her Cheeks a tender shower did glide,
The Trophies of my Victory, Joy, and Pride:
She yields, ye Gods (I cry'd) and in my Arms,
Gives up the wonderous Treasure of her Charms.
—Transported to the Bower of Bliss we high,
But once more met Respect upon the way,
But not as heretofore with Meen and Grace
All formal, but a gay and smiling Face;
A different sort of Air his looks now wears,
Galljard and Joyful every part appears.
And thus he said—

Go, happy Lovers, perfect the desires,
That fill two Hearts that burn with equal Fires;
Receive the mighty Recompence at last,
Of all the Anxious hours you've past,
Enter the Bower where endless Pleasures flow,
Young Joys, new Raptures all the year:
Respect has nothing now to do,
He always leaves the Lover here.
Young Loves attend and here supply all want,
In secret Pleasures I'm no confident.

Respect here left me: and He scarce was gone,
But I perceiv'd a Woman hasting on,
Naked she came; all lovely, and her Hair
Was loosely flying in the wanton Air:
Love told me 'twas Occasion, and if I
The swift pac'd Maid shou'd pass neglected by,
My Love, my Hopes, and Industry were vain,
For she but rarely e're returned again.
I stopt her speed, and did implore her Aid,

Which granted, she Aminta did perswade
Into the Palace of true Joys to hast,
And thither 'twas, we both arriv'd at last.
Oh Lysidas, no Mortal Sense affords,
No Wit, no Eloquence can furnish Words
Fit for the soft Discription of the Bower;
Some Love-blest God in the Triumphing hour,
Can only guess, can only say what 'tis;
Yet even that God but faintly wou'd express,
Th' unbounded pleasures of the Bower of Bliss.
A slight, a poor Idea may be given,
Like that we fancy when we paint a Heav'n,
As solid Christal, Diamonds, shining Gold,
May fancy Light, that is not to be told.
To vulgar Senses, Love like Heaven shou'd be
(To make it more Ador'd) a Mystery:
Eternal Powers! when ere I sing of Love,
And the unworthy Song immortal prove;
To please my wandering Ghost when I am Dead,
Let none but Lovers the soft stories read;
Praise from the Wits and Braves I'le not implore;
Listen, ye Lovers all, I ask no more;
That where Words fail, you may with thought supply,
If ever any lov'd like me, or were so blest as I.

The Prospect and Bower of Bliss.

I.
'Tis all eternal Spring around,
And all the Trees with fragrant flowers are Crown'd;
No Clouds, no misty Showers obscure the Light,
But all is calm, serene and gay,
The Heavens are drest with a perpetual bright,
And all the Earth with everlasting May.
Each minute blows the Rose and Jesamine,
And twines with new-born Eglantine,
Each minute new Discoveries bring;
Of something sweet, of something ravishing.

II.
Fountains, wandering Brooks soft rills,
That o're the wanton Pebbles play;
And all the Woods with tender murmuring fills,
Inspiring Love, inciting Joy;
(The sole, the solemn business of the day)
Through all the Groves, the Glades and thickets run,
And nothing see but Love on all their Banks along;

A thousand Flowers of different kinds,
The neighbouring Meads adorn;
Whose sweetness snatcht by flying Winds,
O're all the Bow'r of Bliss is born;
Whether all things in nature strive to bring,
All that is soft, all that is ravishing.

III.
The verdant Banks no other Prints retain,
But where young Lovers, and young Loves have lain.
For Love has nothing here to do,
But to be wanton, soft and gay,
And give a lavish loose to joy.
His emptied Quiver, and his Bow,
In flowry Wreaths with rosy Garlands Crown'd,
In Myrtle shades are hung,
As Conquerors when the Victories won,
Dispose their glorious Trophies all around.
Soft Winds and Eccho's that do haunt each Grove,
Still whisper, and repeat no other Songs than Love.
Which round about the sacred Bower they sing,
Where every thing arrives that's sweet and ravishing.

IV.
A thousand gloomy Walks the Bower contains,
Sacred all to mighty Love;
A thousand winding turns where Pleasure reigns;
Obscur'd from day by twining Boughs above,
Where Love invents a thousand Plays,
Where Lovers act ten thousand Joys:
Nature has taught each little Bird,
A soft Example to afford;
They Bill and Look, and Sing and Love,
And Charm the Air, and Charm the Grove;
Whilst underneath the Ravisht Swain is lying,
Gazing, Sighing, Pressing, Dying;
Still with new desire warm'd,
Still with new Joy, new Rapture charm'd;
Amongst the green soft Rivulets do pass,
In winding Streams half hid in Flowers and Grass,
Who Purl and Murmur as they glide along,
And mix their Musick with the Shepherds Pipe and Song,
Which Eccho's through the sacred Bower repeat,
Where every thing arrives that's ravishing and sweet.

V.
The Virgin here shows no disdain,
Nor does the Shepherd Sigh in vain,

This knows no Cruelty, nor that no Pain:
No Youth complains upon his rigorous fair;
No injur'd Maid upon her perjur'd dear,
'Tis only Love, fond Love finds entrance here;
The Notes of Birds, the Murmuring Boughs,
When gentle Winds glide through the Glades,
Soft Sighs of Love, and soft breath'd Vows,
The tender Whisperings of the yielding Maids,
Dashing Fountains, Purling Springs,
The short breath'd crys from faint resistance sent,
(Crys which no aid desires or brings)
The soft effects of Fear and Languishment;
The little struggling of the fair,
The trembling force of the young Conqueror,
The tender Arguments he brings,
The pretty Non-sence with which she assails.
Which as she speaks, she hopes it nought prevails
But yielding owns her Love above her Reasonings,
Is all is heard: Silence and shade the rest.
Which best with Love, which best with Joys consist,
All which young Eccho's through the Bower does sing,
Where every thing is heard, that's sweet and ravishing.

VI.
Recesses Dark, and Grotto's all conspire,
To favour Love and soft desire;
Shades, Springs and Fountains flowry Beds,
To Joys invites, to Pleasure leads,
To Pleasure which all Humane thought exceeds.
Heav'n, Earth, and Sea, here all combine,
To propagate Love's great design,
And render the Appointments all Divine.
After long toyl, 'tis here the Lover reaps
Transporting softnesses beyond his hopes;
'Tis here fair Eyes, all languishing impart
The secrets of the fond inclining Heart;
Fine Hands and Arms for tender Pressings made,
In Love's dear business always are imploy'd:
The soft Inchantments of the Tongue,
That does all other Eloquence controul,
Is breath'd with broken Sighs among,
Into the Ravish'd Shepherds Soul,
Whilst all is taken, all is given,
That can compleat a Lovers Heav'n:
And Io Peans through the Woods do ring,
From new fletch'd God, in Songs all Ravishing.

Oh my dear Lysidas! my faithful Friend,

Would I cou'd here with all my Pleasures end:
'Twas Heaven! 'twas Extaxsie! each minute brought
New Raptures to my Senses, Soul and Thought;
Each Look, each Touch, my Ravisht fancy charm'd,
Each Accent of her Voice my Blood Alarm'd;
I pant with every Glance, faint with a Kiss,
Oh Judge my Transports then in higher Bliss.
A while all Dead, between her Arms I lay,
Unable to possess the conquer'd Joys;
But by degrees my Soul its sense retriev'd;
Shame and Confusion let me know I liv'd.
I saw the trembling dis-appointed Maid,
With charming angry Eyes my fault upbraid,
While Love and Spight no kind Excuse affords,
My Rage and Softness was above dull Words,
And my Misfortune only was exprest,
By Signing out my Soul into her Brest:
A thousand times I breath'd Aminta's name,
Aminta! call'd! but that increas'd my flame.
And as the Tide of Love flow'd in, so fast
My Low, my Ebbing Vigor out did hast.
But 'twas not long, thus idly, and undone
I lay, before vast Seas came rowling on,
Spring-tides of Joy, that the rich neighboring shoar
And down the fragrant Banks it proudly bore,
O're-flow'd and ravisht all great Natures store.
Swoln to Luxurious heights, no bounds it knows,
But wantonly it Triumphs where it flows.
Some God inform Thee of my blest Estate,
But all their Powers divert thee from my Fate.
'Twas thus we liv'd the wonder of the Groves,
Fam'd for our Love, our mutual constant Loves.
Young Amorous Hero's at her Feet did fall,
Despair'd and dy'd, whilst I was Lord of All;
Her Empire o're my Soul each moment grew,
New Charms each minute did appear in view,
And each appointment Ravishing and New.
Fonder each hour my tender Heart became,
And that which us'd t' allay, increas'd my Flame.
But on a day, oh may no chearful Ray,
Of the Sun's Light, bless that succeeding day!
May the black hours from the account be torn,
May no fair thing upon thy day be born!
May fate and Hell appoint thee for their own,
May no good deed be in thy Circle done!
May Rapes, Conspiricies and Murders stay,
Till thou com'st on, and hatch em in thy day!
—'Twas on this day all Joyful Gay and Fair,

Fond as desire, and wanton as the Air;
Aminta did with me to the blest Bower repair.
Beneath a Beechy Shade, a flowry Bed,
Officious Cupid's for our Pleasure spred,
Where never did the Charmer ere impart,
More Joy, more Rapture to my ravisht Heart:
'Twas all the first; 'twas all beginning Fire!
'Twas all new Love! new Pleasure! new Desire!
—Here stop, my Soul—
Stop thy carreer of Vanity and Pride,
And only say,—'Twas here Aminta dy'd:
The fleeting Soul as quickly dis-appears,
As leaves blown off with Winds, or falling Stars;
And Life its flight assum'd with such a pace;
It took no farewel of her lovely Face,
The Fugitive not one Beauty did surprize,
It scarce took time to languish in her Eyes,
But on my Bosom bow'd her charming Head;
And sighing, these surprizing words she said:
"Joy of my Soul, my faithful tender Youth,
Lord of my Vows, and Miracle of Truth:
Thou soft obliger—: of thy Sex the best,
Thou blessing too Extream to be possest;
The Angry God, designing we must part,
Do render back the Treasure of thy Heart;
When in some new fair Breast, it finds a room,
And I shall ly—neglected—in my Tomb—
Remember—oh remember—the fair she,
Can never love thee, darling Youth, like me."
Then with a Sigh she sunk into my Brest,
While her fair Eyes her last farewel exprest;
To aiding God's I cry'd; but they were Deaf,
And no kind pow'r afforded me relief:
I call her name, I weep, I rave and faint,
And none but Eccho's answer my Complaint;
I Kiss and Bathe her stiffening Face with Tears,
Press it to mine, as cold and pale as her's;
The fading Roses of her Lips I press,
But no kind Word the silenc'd Pratlers will confess;
Her lovely Eyes I kiss, and call upon,
But all their wonted answering Rhetorick's gone.
Her charming little Hands in vain I ask,
Those little Hands no more my Neck shall grasp;
No more about my Face her Fingers play,
Nor brede my Hair, or the vain Curls display,
No more her Tongue beguiling Stories tell,
Whose wonderous Wit cou'd grace a Tale so well;
All, all is fled, to Death's cold Mansion gone,

And I am left benighted and undone,
And every day my Fate is hasting on.
From the inchanting Bower I madly fly,
That Bower that now no more affords me Joy.
Love had not left for me one Bliss in store,
Since my Aminta you'd dispence no more.
—Thence to a silent Desert I advance,
And call'd the Desert of Remembrance;
A solitude upon a Mountain plac'd,
All gloomy round, and wonderous high and vast,
From whence Love's Island all appears in view,
And distant Prospects renders near and true;
Each Bank, each Bower, each dear inviting Shade,
That to our Sacred Loves was conscious made;
Each flowry Bed, each Thicket and each Grove,
Where I have lain Charm'd with Aminta's Love;
(Where e're she chear'd the day, and blest the Night)
Eternally are present to my Sight.
Where e're I turn, the Landskip does confess,
Something that calls to mind past happiness.
This, Lysidas, this is my wretched state,
'Tis here I languish, and attend my Fate.
But e're I go, 'twou'd wonderous Pleasure be,
(If such a thing can e're arrive to me)
To find some Pity (Lysidas) from thee.
Then I shou'd take the Wing, and upwards fly,
And loose the Sight of this dull World with Joy.

Your Lysander.

LYCIDUS: OR, THE LOVER IN FASHION, &c.

To the EARL OF MELFORD, &c., Knight of the most Noble Order of the Thistle.

My Lord,

This Epistle Dedicatory which humbly lays this Little Volume at your Lordships feet, and begs a Protection there, is rather an Address than a Dedication; to which a great many hands have subscrib'd, it Presenting your Lordship a Garland whose Flowers are cull'd by several Judgments in which I claim the least part; whose sole Ambition is this way to congratulate your Lordships new Addition of Honour, that of the Most Noble Order of the Thistle, an Honour which preced's that of the Garter, having been supported by a long Race of Kings, and only fell with the most Illustrious of Queens, whose memory (which ought to be Establish'd, in all hearts can not be better preserv'd,) than by reviving this so Ancient Order; well has His Majesty chosen its Noble Champions, among whom none merits more the Glory of that Royal Favor than your Lordship: whose Loyalty to His Sacred Person and interest through all the adversities of Fate, has begot you so perfect a veneration in all hearts, and is so peculiarly the Innate vertue of your Great mind; a virtue not shewn by unreasonable fits when it shall serve an end, (a false Bravery for a while when least needful, and thrown off when put to useful Tryal; like those who weighing Advantages by Probabilities only, and fancying the future to out-poyse the present, cast there their Anchor of Hope,) but a virtue built on so sure and steady Basis's of Honour, as nothing can move or shake; the Royal Interest being so greatly indeed the Property of Nobility, and so much even above life and Fortune: Especially when to support a Monarch so truly just, so wise and great; a Monarch whom God Almighty Grant long to Reign over Us, and still to be serv'd by men of Principles so truly Brave, as those that shine in your Lordship.

Pardon, my Lord, this Digression and the meanness of this Present, which to a Person of your Lordships great and weighty Employments in the world may seem Improper, if I did not know that the most Glorious of States-men must sometimes unbend from Great Affairs, and seek a diversion in trivial Entertainments; Though Poetry will Justle for the Preeminency of all others, and I know is not the least in the Esteem of your Lordship, who is so admirable a Judge of it, if any thing here may be found worthy the Patronage it Implores, 'twill be a sufficient Honour to,

My Lord,
Your Lordships most humble,
most oblig'd,
and obedient Servant,
A. BEHN.

To Mrs. B. on her Poems.

Hail, Beauteous Prophetess, in whom alone,
Of all your sex Heav'ns master-piece is shewn.
For wondrous skill it argues, wondrous care,
Where two such Stars in firm conjunction are,
A Brain so Glorious, and a Face so fair.
Two Goddesses in your composure joyn'd,
Nothing but Goddess cou'd, you're so refin'd,
Bright Venus Body gave, Minerva Mind.

How soft and fine your manly numbers flow,
Soft as your Lips, and smooth as is your brow.
Gentle as Air, bright as the Noon-days Sky,
Clear as your skin, and charming as your Eye.
No craggy Precipice the Prospect spoyles,
The Eye no tedious barren plain beguiles.
But, like Thessalian Feilds your Volumes are,
Rapture and charms o're all the soyl appear,
Astrea and her verse are Tempe every where.

Ah, more than Woman! more than man she is,
As Phæbus bright; she's too, as Phæbus wise.
The Muses to our sex perverse and coy
Astrea do's familiarly enjoy.

She do's their veiled Glorys understand,
And what we court with pain, with ease command.
Their charming secrets they expanded lay,
Reserv'd to us, to her they all display.
Upon her Pen await those learned Nine.
She ne're but like the Phosph'rus draws a line,
As soon as toucht her subjects clearly shine.

The femal Laurels were obscur'd till now,
And they deserv'd the Shades in which they grew:
But Daphne at your call return's her flight,
Looks boldly up and dares the God of light.
If we Orinda to your works compare,
They uncouth, like her countrys soyle, appear,
Mean as its Pesants, as its Mountains bare:
Sappho tasts strongly of the sex, is weak and poor,
At second hand she russet Laurels wore,
Yours are your own, a rich and verdant store.
If Loves the Theme, you out-do Ovid's Art,
Loves God himself can't subtiller skill impart,
Softer than's plumes, more piercing than his Dart.

If Pastoral be her Song, she glads the Swains
With Livelier notes, with spritelier smiles the plains.
More gayly than the Springs she decks the Bowrs
And breaths a second May to Fields and Flowrs.
If e're the golden Age again return
And flash in shining Beames from's Iron Urn,
That Age not as it was before shall be,
But as th' Idea is refin'd by thee.
That seems the common; thines the Elixir, Gold,
So pure is thine, and so allay'd the old.

Happy, ye Bards, by fair Astrea prais'd,
If you'r alive, to brighter life you're rais'd;
For cherisht by her Beams you'll loftyer grow,
You must your former learned selves out-do,
Thô you'd the parts of Thirsis and of Strephon too.
Hail, mighty Prophetess! by whom we see
Omnipotence almost in Poetry:
Your flame can give to Graves Promethean fire,
And Greenhill's clay with living paint inspire;
For like some Mystick wand with awful Eyes
You wave your Pen, and lo the dead Arise.

Kendrick.

LYCIDUS:

or, the Lover in Fashion, &c.

I Have receiv'd your melancholy Epistle, with the Account of your Voyage to the Island of Love; of your Adventures there, and the Relation of the death of your Aminta: At which you shall forgive me if I tell you I am neither surpris'd nor griev'd, but hope to see you the next Campagne, as absolutely reduc'd to reason as myself. When Love, that has so long deprived you of Glory, shall give you no more Sighs but at the short remembrances of past Pleasures; and that after you have heard my Account of the Voyage I made to the same place, with my more lucky one back again, (for I, since I saw you, have been an Adventurer) you will by my Example become of my Opinion, (notwithstanding your dismal Tales of Death and the eternal Shades,) which is, that if there be nothing that will lay me in my Tomb till Love brings me thither, I shall live to Eternity.

I must confess 'tis a great Inducement to Love, and a happy Advance to an Amour, to be handsom, finely shap'd, and to have a great deal of Wit; these are Charms that subdue the Hearts of all the Fair: And one sees but very few Ladies, that can resist these good Qualities, especially in an Age so gallant as ours, yet all this is nothing if Fortune do not smile: And I have seen a Man handsom, well shap'd, and of a great deal of Wit, with the advantage of a thousand happy Adventures, yet finds himself in the end, fitter for an Hospital than the Elevation of Fortune: And the Women are not contented we should give them as much Love as they give us, (which is but reasonable,) but they would compel us all to Present and Treat 'em lavishly, till a Man hath consumed both Estate and Body in their Service. How many do we see, that are wretched Examples of this Truth, and who have nothing of all they enjoyed remaining with 'em, but a poor Idæa of past Pleasures, when rather the Injury the Jilt has done 'em, ought to be eternally present with 'em. Heaven keep me from being a Woman's Property. There are Cullies enough besides you or I, Lysander.

One would think now, That I, who can talk thus Learnedly and Gravely, had never been any of the number of those wretched, whining, sighing, dying Fops, I speak of, never been jilted and cozen'd of both my Heart and Reason; but let me tell those that think so, they are mistaken, and that all this Wisdom and Discretion, I now seem replenish'd with, I have as dearly bought as any keeping Fool of 'em all. I was Li'd and flattered into Wit, jilted and cozen'd into Prudence, and, by ten thousand broken Vows and perjured Oaths, reduced to Sense again; and can laugh at all my past Follies now.

After I have told you this, you may guess at a great part of my Story; which, in short, is this: I would needs make a Voyage, as you did, to this fortunate Isle, and accompanyed with abundance of young Heirs, Cadets, Coxcombs, Wits, Blockheads, and Politicians, with a whole Cargo of Cullies all, nameless and numberless we Landed on the Inchanted Ground; the first I saw, and lik'd, was charming Silvia; you believe I thought her fair as Angels; young, as the Spring, and sweet as all the Flowers the blooming Fields produce; that when she blush'd, the Ruddy Morning open'd, the Rose-buds blew, and all the Pinks and Dazies spread; that when she sigh'd or breath'd, Arabia's Spices, driven by gentle Winds, perfum'd all around; that when she look'd on me, all Heaven was open'd in her Azure Eyes, from whence Love shot a thousand pointed Darts, and wounded me all over; that when she spoke, the Musick of the Spheres, all that was ravishing in Harmony, blest the Adoring Listener; that when she walk'd, Venus in the Mirtle Grove when she advanced to meet her lov'd Adonis, assuming all the Grace young Loves cou'd give, had not so much of Majesty as Silvia: In fine, she did deserve, and I compared her to all the Fopperies, the Suns, the Stars, the Coral, and the Pearl, the Roses and Lillies, Angels Spheres, and Goddesses, fond Lovers dress their Idols in. For she was all, fancy and fine imagination could adorn her with, at least, the gazing Puppy thought so. 'Twas such I saw and lov'd; but knowing I did Adore, I made my humble Court, and she, by all my trembling, sighings, pantings, the going and returning of my Blood, found all my Weakness and her own Power; and using all the Arts of her Sex, both to ingage and secure me, play'd all the Woman over: She wou'd be scornful and kind by turns, as she saw convenient, This to check my Presumption and too easy hope; That to preserve me from the brink of despair. Thus was I tost in the Blanket of Love, sometimes up, and sometimes down, as her Wit and Humour was in or out of tune, all which I watch'd, and waited like a Dog, that still the oftner kick'd wou'd fawn the more.

Oh, 'tis an excellent Art this managing of a Coxcomb, the Serpent first taught it our Grandam Eve: and Adam was the first kind Cully: E're since they have kept their Empire over Men, and we have, e're since, been Slaves. But I, the most submissive of the whole Creation, was long in gaining Grace; she used me as she meant to keep me, Fool enough for her Purpose. She saw me young enough to do her Service, handsom enough to do her Credit, and Fortune enough to please her Vanity and Interest: She therefore suffer'd me to Love, and Bow among the Crowd, and fill her Train. She gave me hope enough to secure me too, but gave me nothing else, till she saw me languish to that degree, she feared, to lose the Glory of my Services, by my death; only this Pleasure kept me alive, to see her treat all my Rivals with the greatest Rigour imaginable, and to me all sweetness, exposing their foibles; and having taken Notice of my Languishment, she suffered me Freedoms that wholly Ravish'd me, and gave me hopes I shou'd not be long a dying for all she cou'd give.

But, since I have a great deal to say of my Adventures in passing out of this Island of Love: I will be as brief as I can in what arrived to me on the Place; and tell you, That after Ten thousand Vows of eternal Love on both sides, I had the Joy, not only to be believ'd and lov'd, but to have her put herself into my Possession, far from all my Rivals: Where, for some time I lived with this charming Maid, in all the Raptures of Pleasure, Youth, Beauty, and Love could create. Eternally we loved, and lived together, no day nor night separated us, no Frowns interrupted our Smiles, no Clouds our Sun-shine; the Island was all perpetual Spring, still flowery and green, in Bowers, in Shades, by purling Springs and Fountains, we past our hours, unwearied and uninterrupted. I cannot express to you the happy Life I led, during this blessed Tranquility of Love, while Silvia still was pleased and still was gay. We walked all day together in the Groves, and entertained ourselves with a thousand Stories of Love; we laught at the foolish World, who could not make their Felicity without Crowds and Noise: We pitied Kings in Courts in this Retirement, so well we liked our Solitude; till on a day, (blest be that joyful day, though then 'twas most accurst,) I say upon that day, I know not by what accident I was parted from my Charmer, and left her all alone, but in my absence, there incountred her a Woman extremely ugly, and who was however very nice and peevish, inconstant in her temper, and no one place could continue her: The finest things in the World were troublesom to her, and she was Shagreen at every thing; her Name is Indifference; she is a Person of very great Power in this Island, (though possibly you never incountred her there,) and those that follow her, depart from the Isle of Love without any great pains. She brought Silvia to the Lake of Disgust, whether, in persuing her (at my return,) I found her, ready to take Boat to have past quite away, and where there are but too many to transport those Passengers, who follow Indifference over the Lake of Disgust. I saw this disagreeable Creature too, but she appeared too ugly for me to approach her, but forcing Silvia back, I returned again to the Palace of True Pleasure, where some days after there arrived to me a Misfortune, of which, I believed I should never have seen an end. I found Silvia inviron'd round with new Lovers, still adoring and pleasing her a thousand ways, and though none of 'em were so rich, so young, or so handsom as I, she nevertheless failed not to treat 'em with all the Smiles and Caresses 'twas possible to imagin; when I complain'd of this, she would satisfy my fears with so many Vows and Imprecations, that I would believe her, and think myself unreasonable, but when she would be absent whole days, in a hundred places, she would find such probable Excuse, and lye with such a Grace, no mortal cou'd have accused her, so that all the whole Island took notice that I was a baffled Cuckold, before I could believe she would deceive me, so heartily she damn'd herself: Through all the Groves I was the pointed Coxcomb, laught at aloud, and knew not where the jest lay; but thought myself as secure in the Innocence of my deceiving fair one, as the first hour I Charmed her, and like a keeping Cully, lavish'd out my Fortune, my plenteous Fortune, to make her fine to Cuckold me. 'Sdeath! how I scorn the Follies of my Dotage; and am resolv'd to persue Love for the future, in such a manner as it shall never cost me a Sigh: This shall be my method.

A Constancy in Love I'll prise,
And be to Beauty true:
And doat on all the lovely Eyes,
That are but fair and new.
On Cloris Charms to day I'll feed,
To morrow Daphne move;
For bright Lucinda next I'll bleed,
And still be true to Love.

But Glory only and Renown
My serious hours shall charm;
My Nobler Minutes those shall Crown,
My looser hours, my Flame.
All the Fatigues of Love I'll hate,
And Phillis's new Charms
That hopeless Fire shall dissipate,
My Heart for Cloe warms.

The easie Nymph I once enjoy'd
Neglected now shall pass,
Possession, that has Love destroy'd
Shall make me pitiless.
In vain she now attracts and mourns,
Her moving Power is gone,
Too late (when once enjoy'd,) she burns,
And yeilding, is undone.

My Friend, the little charming Boy
Conforms to my desires,
And 'tis but to augment my Joy
He pains me with his Fires;
All that's in happy Love I'll tast,
And rifle all his store,
And for one Joy, that will not last,
He brings a thousand more.

Perhaps, my Friend, at this Account of my Humor you may smile, but with a reasonable consideration you will commend it, at least, though you are not so wise as to persue my Dictates. Yet I know you will be diverted with my Adventures; though there be no love in 'em that can resemble 'em to yours. Take then the History of my Heart, which I assure you, boasts itself of the Conquests it has made.

A thousand Martyrs I have made,
All sacrific'd to my desire;
A thousand Beauties have betray'd,
That languish in resistless Fire.
The untam'd Heart to hand I brought,
And fixt the wild and wandring Thought.

I never vow'd nor sigh'd in vain
But both, thô false, were well receiv'd.
The Fair are pleas'd to give us pain,
And what they wish is soon believ'd.
And thô I talk'd of Wounds and Smart,
Loves Pleasures only toucht my Heart.

Alone the Glory and the Spoil
I always Laughing bore away;
The Triumphs, without Pain or Toil,
Without the Hell, the Heav'n of Joy.
And while I thus at random rove
Despise the Fools that whine for Love.

I was a great while, (like you,) before I forgot the remembrance of my first Languishments, and I almost
thought (by an excess of Melancholy,) that the end of my Misfortunes were with my Life at hand: Yet
still like a fond Slave, willing to drag my Fetters on, I hop'd she would find Arguments to convince me
she was not false; and in that Humor, fear'd only I should not be handsomly and neatly jilted. Could she
but have dissembled well, I had been still her Cully. Could she have play'd her Game with discretion, but,
vain of her Conquest, she boasted it to all the World, and I alone was the kind keeping Blockhead, to
whom 'twas unperceived, so well she swore me into belief of her Truth to me. Till one day, lying under a
solitary Shade, with my sad Thoughts fixt on my declining Happiness, and almost drown'd in Tears, I saw
a Woman drest in glorious Garments, all loose and flowing with the wind, scouring the Fields and Groves
with such a pace, as Venus, when she heard her lov'd Youth was slain, hasted to behold her ruin. She
past me, as I lay, with an unexpressible swiftness, and spoke as she run, with a loud Voice. At her first
approach, I felt a strange trembling at my Heart without knowing the reason, and found at last this
Woman was Fame. Yet I was not able to tell from whence proceeded my Inquietude. When her Words
made me but too well understand the Cause: The fatal Subject of what she cry'd, in passing by me, were
these:

Poor Lycidus, for shame arise,
And wipe Loves Errors from thy Eyes;
Shake off the God that holds thy Heart;
Since Silvia for another burns,
And all thy past Indurement scorns
While thou the Cully art.

I believed, as she spoke, that I had ill understood her, but she repeated it so often, that I no longer
doubted my wretchedness. I leave you, who so well can guess, to imagin, what Complaints I made, filling
the Grove, where I was laid, with my piteous Cries; sometimes I rose and raved, and rail'd on Love, and

reproached the fair Fugitive. But the tender God was still pleading in my Heart, and made me ever end my noisy Griefs in Sighs and silent Tears. A thousand Thoughts of revenge I entertained against this happy Rival, and the charming ingrate: But those Thoughts, like my Rage, would also end in soft reproaching murmurs and regret only. And I would sometimes argue with Love in this manner.

Ah, cruel Love! when will thy Torments cease?
And when shall I have leave to dye in Peace?
And why, too charming and too cruel Maid,
Cou'd'st thou not yet thy fleeting Heart have stay'd?
And by degrees thy fickle Humor shewn,
By turns the Enemy and Friend put on:
Have us'd my Heart a little to thy scorn,
The loss at least might have been easier born.
With feigned Vows, (that poor Expence of Breath,)
Alas thou might'st have sooth'd me to my death.
Thy Coldness, and thy visible decays
In time had put a period to my days.
And lay'd me quietly into my Tomb,
Before thy proof of Perjuries had come.
You might have waited yet a little space
And sav'd mine, and thy, Honour this disgrace;
Alas I languish'd and declin'd apace.
I lov'd my Life too eagerly away
To have disturb'd thee with too long a stay.
Ah! cou'd you not my dying Heart have fed
With some small Cordial Food, till I was dead?
Then uncontroul'd, and unreproach'd your Charms
Might have been render'd to my Rival's Arms.
Then all my right to him you might impart,
And Triumph'd o're a true and broken Heart.

Though I complained thus for a good while, I was not without some secret hope, that what I had heard was not true; nor would I be persuaded to undeceive myself of that hope which was so dear and precious to me. I was not willing to be convinced I was intirely miserable, out of too great a fear to find it true; and there were some Moments in which I believed Fame might falsly accuse Silvia, and it did not seem reasonable to me, that, after all the Vows and Oaths she had made, she should so easily betray 'em, and forgetting my Services, receive those of another, less capable of rend'ring them to her advantage. Sometimes I would excuse her ingratitude with a thousand things that seem'd reasonable, but still that was but to make me more sensible of my disgrace; and then I would accuse myself of a thousand weaknesses below the Character of a Man; I would even despise and loath my own easiness, and resolve to be no longer a Mark-out-fool for all the Rhiming Wits of the Island to aim their Dogrel at. And grown, as I imagined, brave at this thought, I resolved first to be fully convinced of the perfidy of my Mistress, and then to rent my Heart from the attachment that held it.

You know, that from the Desart of Remembrance, one does, with great facility, look over all the Island of Love. I was resolved to go thither one day; and where indeed I could survey all things that past, in the Groves, the Bowers, by Rivers, or Fountains, or whatever other place, remote or obscure 'twas from thence, that one day I saw the faithless Silvia, in the Palace of True Pleasure, in the very Bower of Bliss with one of my Rivals, but most intimate Friend.

'Twas there, I saw my Rival take
Pleasures, he knew how to make;
There he took, and there was given,
All the Joys that Rival Heaven;
Kneeling at her Feet he lay,
And in transports dy'd away:
Where the faithless suffer'd too
All the amorous Youth cou'd do.

The Ardour of his fierce desire
Set his Face and Eyes on fire.
All their Language was the Blisses
Of Ten thousand eager Kisses;
While his ravish'd Neck she twin'd
And to his Kisses, Kisses join'd;
Till, both inflam'd, she yeilded so
She suffer'd all the Youth cou'd do.

In fine, 'twas there I saw that I must lose the day. And I saw in this Lover Ten thousand Charms of Youth and Beauty; on which the ingrate with greedy languishing Eyes, eternally gazed with the same Joy she used to behold me when she made me most happy. I confess, this Object was so far from pleasing me, (as I believed a confirmation would,) that the change inspired me with a rage, which nothing else could do, and made me say things unbecoming the Dignity of my Sex, who ought to disdain those faithless Slaves, which Heaven first made to obey the Lords of the Creation. A thousand times I was about to have rush'd upon 'em, and have ended the Lives of the loose betrayers of my repose, but Love stepp'd in and stay'd my hand, preventing me from an Outrage, that would have cost me that rest of Honour, I yet had left: But when my rage was abated, I fell to a more insupportable Torment, that of extream Grief to find another possest of what I had been so long, and with so much Toil in gaining: 'Twas thus I retir'd, and after a little while brought myself to make calm Reflections upon this Adventure, which reduced me to some reason. When one day as I was walking in an unfrequented Shade, whither my Melancholy had conducted me, I incountred a Man, of a haughty look and meen, his Apparel rich and glorious, his Eyes awful, and his Stature tall; the very sight of him inspired me with coldness, which render'd me almost insensible of the infidelity of Silvia. This Person was Pride, who looking on me, as he past, with a fierce and disdainful Smile, over his Shoulder, and regarding me with scorn, said;

Why shou'd that faithless wanton give
Thy Heart so mortal pain,
Whose Sighs were only to deceive,
Her Oaths all false and vain?
Despise those Tears thou shedd'st for her,
Disdain to sigh her Name.
To Love, thy Liberty prefer;
To faithless Silvia, Fame.

I knew by his words he was Pride, or Disdain, and would have embraced him; but he put me off, seeing Love still by me, who had not yet abandoned me, and turned himself from me with a regardless scorn, but I, who was resolved not to forsake so discreet a Counsellor, rather chose to take my leave of little Love; who had ever accompanyed me in this Voyage. But oh! this adieu was not taken so easily and soon as I imagined. Love was not to be quitted without abundance of Sighs and Tears at parting, he had been a Witness to all my Adventures, my Confident in this Amour, and not to be deserted without a great deal of pain; I stayed so long in bidding the dear Boy adieu, that I had almost forgot Disdain; at last, though my Heart were breaking to part with the dear fondling, I was resolved and said;

Farewel, my little charming Boy!
Farewel, my fond delight,
My dear Instructor all the day,
My soft repose at night.
Thou, whom my Soul has so carest,
And my poor Heart has held so fast,
Thou never left me in my pain,
Nor in my happier hours;
Thou eas'd me when I did complain,
And dry'd my falling showrs.
When Silvia frown'd still thou woud'st smile,
And all my Cares and Griefs beguile.

But Silvia's gone, and I have torn
Her Witchcrafts from my Heart;
And nobly fortify'd by scorn
Her Empire will subvert;
The Laws establish'd there destroy,
And bid adieu to the dear charming Boy.

In quitting Love I was a great while before I could find Disdain, but I, at last, overtook him: He accompanyed me to a Village, where I received a Joy I had not known since my Arrival to the Isle of Love, and which Repose seemed the sweeter because it was new. When I came to this place, I saw all the World Easie, Idle, and at Liberty: This Village is like a Desart, and all the Inhabitants live within themselves, there is only one Gate, by which we enter into it from the Isle of Love.

This place is called Indifference, and takes its Name from a Princess inhabiting there, a Person very fair and well made; but has a Grace and Meen of so little Wit, and seems so inutile and so silly, that it renders her even ridiculous. As soon as I arrived there, I called to my remembrance all those affronts and cheats of Love, that Silvia had put upon me, and which now served for my diversion, and were agreeable thoughts to me; so that I called myself Ten thousand Sots and Fools for resenting 'em; and that I did not heartily despise 'em, laugh at 'em, and make my Pleasure with the false One as well as the rest; for she dissembled well, and for ought I knew, 'twas but dissembled Love she paid my Rivals. But I, forsooth, was too nice a Coxcomb, I cou'd not feed as others did, and be contented with such Pleasures as she cou'd afford, but I must ingross all, and unreasonably believe a Woman of Youth and Wit had not a longer Race of Love to run than to my Arms alone. Well, 'tis now confest I was a Fool, nor could I hinder myself from saying a thousand times a day;

That Coxcomb can ne're be at ease,

While Beauty inslaves his Soul.
'Tis Liberty only can please,
And he that's Fetter'd is an Owl.

I found it very convenient and happy to dis-ingage from Love, and I have wond'red a thousand times at the Follies that God has made me commit: And though I som'times thought on Silvia, I thought her less charming and fair than she was before her fall; and the Humour I now was in represented her no more meriting that Passion I once had for her, and I fancied she had lost all those Graces for which once I lov'd her: In fine, I was so wholly recovered of my disease of Love for Silvia, that I began to be uneasie for want of employing my Addresses; and a change from so violent a Passion to such a degree of coldness, became insupportable to one of my Youth and I natural Gayety; insomuch, that I was seized with a Dulness, or Languishment, and so great a fit of Melancholy, as I had never felt the like; and my Heart, that was so accustomed to Love, was so out of Humour, that it had no Object or Business for thought, that it lost all its Harmony and Wit; it having nothing to excite it to Life and Motion, passing from so vast a degree of tenderness to an unconcern equally extream. I thought it rude, ill-bred, and idle, to live so indifferent and insignificant a Life. And walking perpetually by myself, (or with those of my own Sex, that could not make my diversion,) I sung all day this following Song to a Hum-drum Tune, to myself;

Not to sigh and to be tender,
Not to talk and prattle Love,
Is a Life no good can render,
And insipidly does move:
Unconcern do's Life destroy,
Which, without Love, can know no Joy.

Life, without adoring Beauty,
Will be useless all the day;

Love's a part of Human Duty,
And 'tis Pleasure to obey.
In vain the Gods did Life bestow,
Where kinder Love has nought to do.

What is Life, but soft desires,
And that Soul, that is not made
To entertain what Love inspires,
Oh thou dull immortal Shade?
Thou'dst better part with Flesh and Blood,
Than be, where Life's not understood.

These were my notions of Life; and I found myself altogether useless in the World without Love; methought I had nothing to animate me to Gallant things, without Love, or Women: I had no use of Wit or Youth without the fair, and yet I did not wish wholly to ingage myself neither a second time, having been so ill-treated before by Love: But I found there were ways to entertain one's self agreeably enough without dying or venturing the breaking of a heart for the matter: That there were Beauties to be obtained without the hazard of hanging or drowning one's self: I never had tried, but I found it natural enough to my Humour and Constitution, to flatter and dissemble, swear and lye; I viewed my self in my Glass, and found myself very well recovered from the Ruins my first Amour had made, and believed myself as fit for Conquest, as any Sir Fopling, or Sir Courtly Nice of 'em all. To this fine Person and good Meen and Shape, (as I thought,) I added handsom Dressing, the thing that takes the Heart infinitely above all your other Parts, and thus set out a snare for vain Beauty; I every day went out of the City of Indifference, to see what new Adventures I could meet withal.

One day I incountred a Woman, who, at first sight appeared very agreeable; she had an Air easie, free, and Galliard; such as fails not to take at first view: This was Coquettre, who, the very first time she saw me, Addrest herself to me with very great Complisance and good Humour, and invited me to her Apartment, where she assured me I should not fail to be entertained very agreeably; and at the same time pulling out of her Pocket a Paper, she shewed me these Words written;

Let Love no more your Heart inspire,
Thô Beauty every hour you see;
Pass no farther than desire,
If you'll truly happy be.
Every day fresh Objects view,
And for all have Complisance.
Search all places still for new,
And to all make some Advance;
For where Wit and Youth agree,
There's no Life like Gallantry.

Laura's Heart you may receive,
And to morrow Julia's prise:
Take what young Diana gives,
Pity Lucia when she dies:
Portia's Face you must admire,
And to Clorin's Shape submit,
Phillis Dancing gives you Fire,
Celia's Softness, Clara's Wit.
Thus all at once you may persue,
'Tis too little to Love two.

The powerful smiling God of Hearts
So much tenderness imparts,
You must upon his Altars lay
A thousand Offerings every day:
And so soft is kind desire;
Oh! so Charming is the Fire,
That if nice Adraste scorns,
Gentler Ariadne burns.
Still Another keep in play
(If One refuse,) to give you Joy.

Cease therefore to disturb your Hours,
For having two desires
A Heart can manage two Amours,
And burn with several Fires.

The day has hours enough in store
To visit two or half a score.

I gave her thanks for her good Counsel, and found I needed not much persuasion to follow Coquettre to a City that bears her Name, and I saw over the Gate of the City at my Entrance, these Verses writ in Gold Letters;

The God of Love beholding every day
Slaves from his Empire to depart away;
(For Hearts that have been once with Love fatigu'd,
A second time are ne'r again intrigu'd:
No second Beauty e'r can move
The Soul to that degree of Love;)
This City built, that we might still obey,
Thô we refus'd his Arbitrary Sway:
'Tis here we find a grateful Recompence
For all Loves former Violence;
Tir'd with his Laws we hither come
To meet a kinder softer doom.
'Tis here the God, without the Tyrant, Reigns,
And Laws agreeable ordains;
Here 'tis with Reason and with Wit he Rules,
And whining Passion Ridicules.
No check or bound to Nature gives,
But kind desire rewarded thrives.
Peevish uneasy Pride, the God
Has banish'd from the blest abode:
All Jealousies, all Quarrels cease,
And here Love lives in perfect Peace.

This agreeable description, gave me new desire to enter into the City; where I incountred a thousand fine Persons all gloriously drest, as if they were purposely set out for Conquest: There was nothing omitted of Cost and Gallantry, that might render 'em intirely Charming, and they employ'd all their Arts of Looks and Dress to gain Hearts.

It is, in a word, from these fair Creatures you are to draw your Satisfaction, and 'tis indeed at a dear rate you buy it, yet, notwithstanding the Expence, a world of People persue 'em.

When I came into the City, I was soon perceived to be a Stranger there, and while I was considering whither I should go, or how to address myself to these fair Creatures, a little Coquette Cupid presented himself to me for a kind Instructer; and to explain him, this in a word is his Character:

He is of the same Race with the other Cupids, has the same Mother too, Venus: He wears a Bow and Arrows, like the rest of the young Loves; but he has no Bando, nothing to cover his Eyes, but he sees perfectly; nor has he any Flambeau: And all the Laws of Coquettre he understands and observes exactly.

I had no sooner received the little Charming God, but he instructed me in all the most powerful Arts to please, in all his little wiles and agreeable deceits; all which he admits of as the most necessary

Recourses to that great end of Man, his true diversion: With all which I was so extreamly pleased, that resolving to be his Votary, I followed him to the most delightful place in the World, the City of Gallantry.

Gallantry is a City very magnificent; at the Entrance of the Gate you incounter Liberality, a Woman of great Wit, delicate Conversation and Complisance: This Lady gives her Passport to all that enter, and without which, you cannot pass, or at least, with great difficulty; and then too you pass your time but very ill; and the more Pasports you have, the better you are received from the fair Inhabitants, and pass your time more agreeable with the fine Conversation you meet with in this City. Love told me this, and it was therefore that I took a great many Pasports from this acceptable Person Liberality. But what renders you yet more Favoured by the Fair and the Young who reside at Gallantry, is, to have a delicate soft Wit, an assiduous Address and a tender way of Conversing; but that which best cullies and pleases the Generality of People there, is Liberality and Complisance: This place of so great Divertisement is re-frequented with all the Parties of the best and most amiable Company, where they invent a thousand new Pleasures every day; Feasting, Balls, Comedies, and Sports, Singing and Serenades, are what employs the whole Four and twenty hours.

By the Virtue of my Pasports from Liberality, I was introduced to all the fine Conversations and Places that afford Pleasure and Delight: I had the good Fortune to make Parties, insomuch, that I was soon known to all the Company in the City, and past the day in Feasting, going with the Young and Fair to delightful Villa's, Gardens, or Rivers in Chases, and a thousand things that pleas'd; and the Nights I passed in Serenading, so that I did not give myself time for Melancholy; and yet for all this I was wearied and fatigued; for when once one has tasted of the Pleasure of Loving and being Beloved, all, that comes after that, is but flat and dull; and if one's Heart be not a little inflamed, all things else are insignificant, and make but very slight touches.

I began therefore for all this to be extreamly Shagreen and out of Humour, amidst all these Pleasures, till one lucky day I met with an Adventure, that warmed my Heart with a tender flame which it had not felt since my happy beginning one for Silvia: One day, as I said, I was conducted by my officious Cupid into a Garden very beautiful, where there are a thousand Labyrinths and Arbours, Walks, Grotto's, Groves and Thickets; and where all the Fair and the Gay resorted; 'twas here I incountred a young Beauty called Bellinda; she was well made, and had an admirable meen, an Air of Gayety and Sweetness; but that which charmed me most of all, was her Wit, which was too ingaging for me to defend my Heart against: I found mine immediately submitting to her Conversation, and you may imagine I did not part with her so long as Decency and good Manners permitted me to stay with her, which was as long as any Company was in the place; nor then, till by my importunity I had gained so much upon her to suffer my Visits, which she did with a Condescention that gave me abundance of hope.

I was no sooner gone, but my Cupid, who took care of me, and entertained me to the best Advantage, carried me that Evening to a Ball, where there were a world of Beauties, among the rest one fair as imagination can conceive; she had all the Charmes of Youth and Beauty; though not so much Wit and Air as Bellinda. To this young adorable I made my Court all the time I remained there, and fancied I never found myself so Charmed, I fancied all the Graces had taken up their dwelling in her Divine Face; and that to subdue one so fair and so innocent, must needs be an extream Pleasure: Yet did I not so wholly fix my desires on this lovely Person, but that the Wit of Bellinda shared my Heart with the Beauty and Youth of Bellimante, so was this young Charmer called: I was extreamly well pleas'd to find I could anew take fire; and infinitely more, when I found I should not be subdued by one alone; nor confined to dull Dotage on a single Beauty; but that I was able to attain to the greatest Pleasure, that of Loving two amiable Persons at once: If with two, I hoped I might with Two score if I pleas'd and had occasion; and though at first it seemed to be very strange and improbable to feel a Passion for two, yet I found it true, and could not determin which I had the greatest tenderness for, or inclination to: But 'tis most certain, that this night I found, or thought I found, more for Bellimante, who fired me with every Smile; I confess she wanted that Gayety of Spirit Bellinda had, to maintain that fire she raised: And ever when I was thoughtful a moment, Coquettre (who is ever in all the Conversation, and where she appears very magnificent and with a great Train,) would, smiling, sing softly in my Ear this Song, for she is very Galliard;

Cease to defend your Amorous Heart,
Against a double flame;
Where two may claim an equal Part
Without reproach or shame.
'Tis Love that makes Life's happiness,
And he that best wou'd live
By Love alone must Life caress,
And all his Darts receive.

Coquettre is a Person, that endeavours to please and humour every Body, but of all those who every day fill her Train, she caresses none with that Address and Assiduity as she did me, for I was a new Face, to whom she is ever most obliging and entertaining. However, notwithstanding the Advice of Coquettre, I fancied this young Charmer had engaged all my Soul; and while I gazed on her Beauty, I thought on Bellinda no more; but believed I should wholly devote myself to Bellimante, whose Eyes alone seemed capable to inflame me.

I took my leave with Sighs, and went home extream well pleas'd with this days Adventure. All this Night I slept as well as if no tenderness had toucht my Heart, and though I Lov'd infinitely, it gave me no disturbance; the next morning a thousand pleasant things Bellinda had said to me, came into my mind, and gave me a new inclination to entertain myself with that witty Beauty; and dressing myself in haste with the desire I had to be with her, I went again, the morning being very inviting, to the Garden, where before I had seen her, and was so lucky to encounter her; I found her blush at my approach; which I counted a good Omen of my future happiness; she received me with all the Gayety and Joy good liking and Wit could inspire: Nor was I backward on my part, but addrest myself to her with all imaginable respect, and as much Love in my Eyes as I was able to put on; which, I found, she saw with Pleasure; she had not entertained me half an hour, but I was so absolutely charmed, that I forgot there was a Bellimante in the World.

Thus for several days I lived; every day visiting both these attracting Beauties, and at Night, when I was retired, was not able to inform myself which I liked best: Both were equally beloved, and it was now, that methought I began to tast of true Joy; I found myself in Love without any sort of inquietude; when I was Melancholy, I went to visit Bellinda, and she with her Gayety and Wit would inspire me with good Humour; If I were over-prest with good Company, and too much Conversation and Noise, I would visit Bellimante, who by a certain softness in her discourse, and a natural Languishment in her Eyes and Manners, charmed and calmed me to a reposed tranquillity; so that to make me fortunate in Love, I could not have fixed my desires better: I had too little Love to be wretched, and enough to make my happiness and Pleasure.

After I had past my time awhile thus in Coquettre, this little Love, who was my Guide, carried me to Declaration: I thought then upon the time of my first Arrival on the Isle of Love; and how Respect, that awful hinderer of our Pleasure, prevented me from going to this Place: I urg'd this very argument Respect then made me, to my Coquet Love now, who for answer return'd me nothing but loud laughter; and when I askt his reason, he replied, that Respect did not forbid any to go to Declaration, but those only who knew not how to behave themselves well there, and who were not so well fashion'd and bred as they ought to be, who go thither: And that it was a mere cheat in Respectto conduct people to Love by Discretion, that being much the farthest way about, and under favor to Monsieur Respect he is but a troublesome companion to a Lover, who designs to cure those wounds the fair has given him, and, if he have no better counsellor, he may languish all his life without revealing the secret of his soul to the object belov'd, and so never find redress. But this Sir Formal, (Respect says Love,) is a very great favourite of the Lady's, who is always in fee with them as a Jilt with a Justice; who manages their Fools just as they wou'd have 'em; for it is the most agreeable thing in the World to them, and what the most feeds their vanity, to see at their feet a thousand Lovers sigh, burn, and languish; the fair are never angry to find themselves belov'd, nor ever weary of being Ador'd. I was extreamly pleas'd at this frank Humour of my little Love who told me this, and without much scruple or consideration to Respect I followed him towards Declaration, and in my way he gave me this Advice.

When you Love, or speak of it,
Make no serious matter on't,
'Twill make but subject for her wit
And gain her scorn in lieu of Grant.
Sneeking, whining, dull Grimasses
Pale the Appetite, they'd move;
Only Boys and formal Asses
Thus are Ridicul'd by Love.

While you make a Mystery
Of your Love and awful flame;
Young and tender Hearts will fly,
Frighted at the very name;
Always brisk and gayly court,
Make Love your pleasure not your pain,
'Tis by wanton play and sport
Heedless Virgins you will gain.

By this time we were arriv'd to Declaration, which is a very little Village, since it is only for Passengers to pass thrô, and none live there, the Country is very Perilous, and those that make a false step run a great risque of falling from some precipice: Round about rises a very great mist, and people have much ado to know each other; of these mists there are two sorts: The one on the side of Denial, the other on that of Permission, the first is very disagreeable and draws a very ill consequence with it; the other directs you to a place of intire divertisement, but I had so good a guide that the entrance gave me no trouble at all. When I came to the Village, I found Bellimante, and Bellinda, to whom by turns I told all my heart; and discover'd all its passion or its tenderness which was to me much better.

When to the charming Bellinda I came,
With my heart full of Love and desire,
To gain my wisht end I talkt of a flame,
Of sighing, and dying, and fire,
I swore to her charms that my soul did submit,

And the slave was undone by the force of her Wit.

To fair Bellimante the same tale I told,
And I vow'd and I swore her fair Eyes
No Heart-Ravisht mortal cou'd ever behold
But he panting and languishing Dys,
And while I was vowing, the ardour of youth
Made myself even believe what I swore was all Truth.

I confess to you, my dear Lysander, that it was a great while before I cou'd make myself be believ'd by
Bellinda, or gain any credit upon her heart, she had a great deal of Wit and cou'd see farther into the
designs of her Lovers than those who had not so much, or had had so many vows pay'd them: I perceiv'd
well enough, I was not hated by her, and that she had not a heart wholly insensible; so that I never
quitted her till I had gain'd so much upon her to accompany me to Permission, where for some time we
pass our days very pleasantly; and having so good fortune with Bellinda, I had now a great desire to try
my power over Bellimante: and where indeed, contrary to my expectation, I was not so happy: But she
went from me to Denial; and I was for that hour oblig'd to return again to Bellinda, it was some time I
searcht her in vain, but at last found her at a little Village, extreamly agreeable. There are very few
Inhabitants, but those that are live in perpetual union, yet do not talk much, for they understand one
another with half words: A sign of the Hand, the Head or the Eye, a glance or smile is sufficient to
declare a great part of the Inclination. It is here where the Lover takes all freedoms, without controul,
and says and does all that soft Love can permit: And every day they take and give a secret
Entertainment, speaking a particular Language, which every body does not understand, and none but
Lovers can reply to; in effect, there are as many Languages as there are persons.

The Governess of this Village is very charming to those that are acquainted with her; and as disagreeable
to those that are not; she is a person of a great deal of Wit, and knows all things. She has a thousand
ways to make herself understood, and comprehends all in a moment, that you wou'd or can say to her.

In this place, to divert, we make a thousand pretty sorts of Entertainments; and we have abundance of
Artifices, which signify nothing, and yet they serve to make life Agreeable and Pleasant.

'Twas thus I liv'd at Intelligence; when I understood that Bellimante was retir'd to Cruelty. This news
afflicted me extreamly, but I was not now of a humour to swell the Floods with my tears, or increase the
rude winds with my ruder sighs; to tear my hair and beat my Innocent breast as I us'd in my first Amour
to do. However I was so far concern'd that I made it my business not to lose this insensible fair one, but
making her a visit in spight of her retreat, I reproacht her with cruelty.

Why, fair Maid, are you uneasy,
When a slave designs to please you;
When he at your feet is lying
Sighing, languishing, and dying?
Why do you preserve your charms
Only for offensive Armes?
What the Lover wou'd possess
You maintain but to oppress.
Cease, fair Maid, your cruel sway,
And let your Lover dy a nobler way.

Who the Devil wou'd not believe me as much in love now as I ever was with Silvia: My heart had learnt then all the soft Language of Love which now it cou'd prattle as naturally as its Mother Tongue; and sighing and dying was as ready for my mouth as when it came from my very heart; and cost me nothing to speak; Love being as cheaply made now by me as a barter for a Horse or a Coach; and with as little concern almost: It pleas'd me while I was speaking, and while I believ'd I was gaining the vanity and pleasure of a conquest over an unvanquisht heart. However I cou'd yet perceive no Grist come to my Mill; no heart to my Lure; young as it was, it had a cunning that was harder to deceive than all Bellinda's Wit: And seeing her persist still in her Resolution I left her with a heart, whose pride more than Passion resented the obdurat'ness of this Maid, I went as well compos'd however as I cou'd to Intelligence; and found even some pleasure in the cruelty and charming resistance of Bellimante, since I propos'd to myself an infinite happiness in softening a heart so averse to Love, and which I knew I shou'd compel to yield some time or other with very little pains and force.

Oh! what Pleasure 'tis to find
A coy heart melt by slow degrees;
When to yielding 'tis inclin'd,
Yet her fear a ruin sees.
When her tears do kindly flow,
And her sighs do come and goe.

Oh! how charming 'tis, to meet
Soft resistance from the fair;
When her pride and wishes meet
And by turns increase her care,
Oh! how charming 'tis to know,
She wou'd yield but can't tell how.

Oh! how pretty is her scorn
When confus'd 'twixt Love and shame,
Still refusing (though she burn,)
The soft pressures of my Flame.
Her Pride in her denyal lies,
And mine is in my Victories.

I feigned nevertheless abundance of Grief to find her still persist in her rigorous Cruelty; and I made her believe that all my absent hours I abandoned myself to sorrows and despairs; though Love knows I parted with all those things in Silvia's Arms. But whatever I pretended, to appear at Cruelty and before Bellimante; at Intelligence I was all Galliard and never in better Humour in my Life than when I went to visit Bellinda: I put on the Gravity of a Lover, and beheld her with a Solemn Languishing Look: In fine, I accustomed myself to counterfeit my Humour, whenever I found it convenient for my Advantage: Tears, Vows, and Sighs cost me nothing, and I knew all the Arts to jilt for Love, and could act the dying Lover, whenever it made for my Satisfaction.

He that wou'd precious time improve.
And husband well his hours,
Let him complain and dye for Love,
And spare no Sighs or Showers.

To second which, let Vows and Oaths
Be ready at your will,
And fittest times and seasons chuse,
To shew your cozening skill.

In fine, after I had sufficiently acted the Languishing Lover, for the accomplishment of all my Wishes, I
thought it time to change the Scene, and without having recourse to Pity, I followed all the Counsels of
my Cupid; who told me, that in stead of dying and whining at her Feet, and damning myself to obtain
her Grace, I should affect a Coldness, and an Unconcern; for, Lycidus, assure yourself, said he, there is
nothing a Woman will not do, rather than lose her Lover either from Vanity or Inclination. I thanked
Love for his kind Advice; and to persue it, the next day I drest myself in all the Gayety imaginable: My
Eyes, my Air, my Language, were all changed; and thus fortified with all the put-on indifference in the
World, I made Bellimante a Visit; and after a thousand things all cold and unconcerned, far from Love or
my former Softness, I cried laughing to her;

Cease, cease, that vain and useless scorn,
Or save it for the Slaves that dye;
I in your Flames no longer burn,
No more the whining Fool you fly;
But all your Cruelty defie.

My Heart your Empire now disdains,
And Frown, or Smile, all's one to me:
The Slave has broke his Servial Chains,
And spight of all your Pride is free
From the Tyrannick Slavery.

Be kind or cruel every day,
Your Eyes may wear what dress they please,
'Twill not affect me either way,
Now my fond Heart has found its Peace,
And all my Tears and Sighings cease.

I must confess you're wondrous fair,
And know, to conquer such a Heart;
Is worth an Age of sad despair,
If Lovers Merits were Desert;
But you're unjust as well as fair,
And Love subsists not with despair,
No more than Lovers by the Air.

I've spar'd no Sighs nor Floods of Tears,
Nor any thing to move your Mind,
With sacred Vows I fed your Cares;
But found your rebel Heart unkind,
And Vanity had made you blind.

No more my Knees shall bow before

Those unconcern'd and haughty Eyes,
Nor be so senseless to adore
That Saint, that all my Prayers despise:
No, I contemn your Cruelty
Since in a Humor not do dye.

Having said all this with an Air of Disdain, I, smiling, took my leave, with much less Civility and Respect than I used to do: and hasting to Intelligence, I past my time very well with Bellinda, to whom I paid all my Visits, and omitted nothing that might make Bellimante know I had forgot her: But at the end of some days by a very happy change, she finding more inclination to Love than to Cruelty, banishing all Obstacles in Favour of a Lover, she came to Intelligence; where at first sight she made me some little Reproaches, and that in so soft a manner, that I did not doubt but I had toucht her Heart: I swore a thousand times, that all I had done, was only put on to see if it were possible she could resent it, and force from her Heart some little concern for my supposed loss. At this time I had abundance of Intreagues upon my hands, for it was not with Bellinda and Bellimante, with whom I lived in this manner; and indeed it is impossible to remain at Intelligence and to make a Court but to two Persons only, where there are so many of the Fair and Young. I writ every day several Billets; and received every day as many: I had every day two or three Rendezvous; and one ought to manage matters very discreetly, that neither Party might come to the knowledge of the others concern; and one ought to be a Man of great Address and Subtilty to love more than one securely; and though this gave me some pain, it was nevertheless an Embarrass very agreeable, and in which I could have lived a great while; if Envy, which cannot suffer any Body to be happy in Intelligence, had not arrived there and told a great many things which discovered my Intreagues; so that Bellinda, with whom I had lived there with great Tranquillity a long time, and Bellimante, with whom I was but just beginning to be happy, were both obliged to quit this delightful place, where we enjoyed many happy hours; and they retired till the noise was a little over; and with them all those who had afforded me any hope: If any one of these had stayed, I had been contented well enough and one might have consol'd me for the loss of the other, but in one day to lose all that made my happiness, put me in such a Melancholy, I knew not for the present what to do for myself; but Coquet Love conducted me to a Village, that gave me a new Pleasure: The scituation of it is marvellous, the Fields and the Groves all about it the most pleasant in the World; the Meadows enamel'd with Rivulets, which run winding here and there, and lose themselves in the Thickets and the Woods. In going, Love said to me: In absence it is in vain to abandon yourself to sorrow. Alas! What signifies it to sigh night and day; the Absent does not hear us; nor can the most tender Affliction or Complaint render a Lover happy, unless the Fair One were present to hear all his Moans, then perhaps they might avail. There was reason in what he said, and I was pleas'd and calm'd; and we arrived at the same time at this Village: All the Houses were fine, and pleasant, we saw all the Graces there by Fountains and by Flowery Springs, and all the Objects that could be imagined agreeable; and the least amiable ones, we saw, gave us a Joy! All the World that inhabit there contribute to Diversion; and this place is called Amusement: Amusement is a young Boy, who stops and gazes at every thing that meets his Eyes, and he makes his Pleasure with every Novelty.

As soon as I arrived at this Village I thought to divert myself, as others did; and to hinder my Thoughts from fixing on the loss of my two Mistresses, and to banish from my mind the Chagrins their Absence gave me; withdrawn from the fair Eyes of Bellimante, and the Charming Wit of Bellinda, and to give my sighing Heart a little ease; upon a thousand Objects I formed my desires, and took a thousand Pleasures to divert my Melancholy: And all the time I lived at this dear place, I passed my time without any inquietude; for every day afforded me new Objects to give me new Wishes. And I now expected, without much impatience, the return of Bellinda and Bellimante; nor did I tire myself with writing to 'em every day; and when I did write, to save the expence of thought, the same Billet served both; a thousand little tender things I said of course to both: And sometimes, especially while I was writing, I thought I had rather seen them than have lived at Amusement, but since it was necessary they should be absent, I bore it with all the Patience I could; sometimes we were in a fit of writing very regularly to one another, but on a sudden I received no Letters at all; the reason of this was, they both understood I lived at Amusement, and had retired themselves to the Palace of Spight: I no sooner received this News, but I rendered myself there also; it is a place where there is alwaies abundance of Tumult, Outrage, Quarrels and Noise: And Spight is a Person who eternally gives occasion of Discontent and Broil; causing People often to fall out with those they love most, and to caress those they hate: But the Quarrels she occasions us with those we love, last but a very short season, and Love reconciles those differences that Spight obliges us to make: Tho' 'tis sometime pleasant enough to see those we Love extreamly, and violently, fall into the highest rage, and say a thousand things injurious and unreasonable, and to swear all the Oaths that angry Love and Fury can inspire, never to see or converse with one another again, and in a moment after to grow calm, weep, and reunite; to be perjured on both sides, and become more fond than ever they were.

A Lovers Rage and Jealousie
One short moment do's confess:
How can they long angry be
Whose Hearts are full of tenderness?

In this Place there wou'd be eternal War, but for a person who inhabits there, and is always the Mediator for Peace, 'tis he that assists to accommodate and bring the Lovers together. This is a very honest person, call'd Right Understanding; he brought me to Bellinda, whom I found accompani'd with a Man that made her a thousand caresses; at my approach she made as if she knew me not, which I took in such disdain, that I apply'd myself to Spight, with a design to be reveng'd on this Haughty scorner. In this humour I made a visit to Bellimante but found her as Implacable as Bellinda, whom no excuses, no reason, cou'd reduce to the temper I had once seen her; in a rage, ten times more than I was before, fill'd with disdain and revenge I complain'd of this treatment to my little Love, who immediately led me into a Grove, where the Beauties and the Graces us'd to walk, to consult upon what return to make for my affront; from one place to another we past on till we came to a little Thicket, on the other side of which, by a little Rivulet we cou'd hear, but not see, two persons discoursing; they were women, and one seemed in a violent Rage against her Lover, who had newly offended her, whilst the other strove in vain to reconcile her, but she went on, vowing to revenge herself with the next object she shou'd Encounter that had but Wit, Youth, and fortune enough to Justify her Love, and make her conquest glorious; her resolution agreeing so with mine, and her manner of speaking, gave me new hope and pleasure, and a great curiosity to see her face; I found by her Resentment she was young and of Quality, and that alone was enough to make me resolve upon Addressing myself to her, and the other person had no sooner left her, but I advanced towards her, with as good a grace as I you'd put on; she was a little surprised, and blushing at first, but I soon reconcil'd her to my conversation. I found her handsom enough to ingage me, and she was as well pleased with me as I was with her, both having the same design which was that of revenge, and you may Imagine, our business being the same, our entertainment was not at first extraordinary, but as my cause of Anger was more reasonable than hers, I began to find myself to soften into liking of this new fair one, who was called Cemena, and who, to spight her former Lover, endeavor'd to be seen with me in all the publick places she cou'd, which gave him Infinite torments of Jealousie. One day as I was walking with this Cemena in a place where the young and the fair frequent, Bellinda and Bellimante often passed by us, and saw us both well pleas'd and in good humour; I cou'd perceive their colour goe and come, and that they were as uneasy at this object, as my heart you'd wish, and by their quitting of the place immediately after, I was assured of all my hope, and believed I had gained my Point; at the end of two or three days, one Morning walking alone in the same place I encountered Bellimante, who hap'ned to be attended with her Woman onely; she chang'd colour at my approach, and wou'd have passed me by but I stay'd her by the Robe; and said a thousand things to her that angry Love inspir'd me with, while she on her side did the same, till we had talk'd ourselves by degrees into reason, and good understanding. I found her Resentment to be only the excess of Love, and all those faults are easily forgiven, I immediately threw myself at her Feet, and made her a thousand protestations of my fidelity, and she, in her turn excused herself with all the tenderness imaginable, she made me a thousand new vows and caresses, and forgot nothing that might perswade me that all she did was by Counsel of Spight.

Oh! how soft it is to see
The fair one we believe untrue,
Eager and impatient be
To be reconcil'd anew;
When their little cheats of Love
Shall with reasons be excus'd,
Oh! how soft it is to prove.
With what ease we are abus'd!

When we come to understand
How unjust are all our fears;
And to feel the lovely hand
Wiping from our Eyes the tears.
And a thousand Favours pay
For every drop they kiss away,
Oh! how soft it is to yield,
To the Maid just reconcil'd.

I found this accommodement extreamly agreeable, and it was in these transports the Lovely Bellimante detain'd me for some days without quitting her, but I found too much Joy in a new reconciliation not to endeavour to make one also with Bellinda; as soon then as Bellimante grew a little off my heart by so long a conversation with one and the same Woman, I, on pretence of some affairs, left her extreamly charm'd and satisfi'd, and hasted to Bellinda, who, methought, was now a new Beauty; at least I found her too considerable to lose the Glory of ingaging her intirely; 'tis possible that both these Ladies, being agitated with as little faith as myself, deceiv'd me with the same design as I did them, to make their pleasure only, and thô this very often came into my thoughts, yet it gave me no great inquietude, they dissembl'd well, and I cou'd not see it; I had the satisfaction and the vanity of 'em, that was as much as I desir'd from any of the fair since Silvia toucht my heart, they both swore they lov'd and both fear'd to displease, if they were unfaithful they had a thousand stratagems to hide their infidelity, and took a great deal of care to keep me, which shew'd a value in me above all the rest of my Rivals, and I beheld myself with some Pride and esteem for having so much power; when ever they offended me they had all the Arts to mollify me, and who wou'd be so critically in love as not to be willing to be so well abus'd? For my part I will not be so nice, as to penetrate into their thoughts, to find what wou'd but displease me if found; but content myself with all I see and find that looks like Love at least and good humour. Nay even in their worst I found a thousand pleasures, those of their quarrels which sometimes happen twenty times a day, when every reconciliation is like a new Mistress, so well they strive to please and be reconcil'd.

But all these pleasures did not satisfy me, there were greater yet behind which I had not arriv'd to with these fair charmers, and however I liv'd at Amusement, making a thousand Amours with a hundred of the most Beautiful, still I had a desire to subdue intirely to my pleasure these two the most hard to gain, but now I was pretty well secur'd of both their hearts and yet neither knew they were each others Rivals in mine. They knew one another, convert, and play'd and walkt together, yet so discreet I was in this Amour that neither was jealous of the other, nor suspected I lov'd both with an equal Ardour; when I hap'ned to be with 'em both I carried myself so equally Gallant that both commended my conduct and imagin'd I did it to hide the secret passion I had for herself, and so many little Arts my Coquet Love had taught me I cou'd with ease manage abundance of intrigues at one and the same time.

But as I said, this did not suffice, nor cou'd the fires that some more willing Beauties allay'd, hinder me from wishing and burning and persuing those two fair persons with an Ardor that had no appearance of decay from any others goodness to me, but in my daily visits to 'em I eternally solicited them to suffer me to accompany them to that charming place call'd Favors, which is a very Beautiful Castle rais'd in a Vally. I confest to you that my Coquet Cupid advis'd me not to go, for fear of attaching myself too much to a place so extreamly agreeable; the Mountains, that environ this Castle, are very high and full of hollow Rocks, which made the scituation very sullen. The Castle itself was delicately built, and surrounded with tall Trees, so thick that one cou'd hardly see the Edifice, nor cou'd the Sun-beams dart throw the gloomy shade; and eternal Night seem'd to sit there in awful state and pleasure: For the more obscure this place is and secret from all Eyes, the better and more acceptable it is to all that enter there, and thô this Vally have many inhabitants, it appears to have none at all; because they love solitude, and, banishing all Publick society, content themselves only to be but two in company together; if there be more they are receiv'd with a very ill welcome, for a third Person in this place wou'd destroy the Pleasure and the harmony. The Inhabitants of this Castle never shew themselves but to those that are very importune, and then not every day, the Ladies that command there are many Sisters all of the name of the Castle; and all very fair, and still one more fair than the other, and when you visit 'em you see 'em not all at once but by degrees and the last you behold is the fairest, and by the pleasure you have in seeing one, you desire to see 'em all. For there are no limits to be given to desire, and as they are never seen by any body altogether, it happens very often that you see but one, and you must have address and great assiduity, abstinence, and good fortune to obtain one of these Favors; but the last will cost you much more trouble than all the rest put together, so very fair, so very nice and coy she is: But when once obtain'd she brings you to the Palace of intire Pleasure; which is neighbouring to the Castle of Favors; but I, who wou'd very fain, at once, have brought to this delicate place both Bellinda and Bellimante, found myself extream uneasy, because, as I said, only two can be well entertain'd at a time! I found it against my humour and against the advice of Love to abandon all, and retire with one only, for in decency and good manners, those, who go to this Castle of Favors, are oblig'd to continue there for some time; and I found, I shou'd be extreamly chagrin after a little with one alone; but both were obstinate and wou'd not suffer a third: and having been so very importune with both, I was asham'd to repent and recant all those things I had said, to persuade them to go, thô in my heart I was very ill satisfi'd I had not persu'd the counsel, Love had given me not to go to Favors at all; he foreseeing an inconvenience in such a retreat, which I, with all my young desires about me and fond of novelty, cou'd not, so well as he, discern; however I had propos'd it with some ardency and wou'd not go back, but resolv'd to make the best advantage of my voyage, and wou'd not declare my regreet till I cou'd no longer hinder it: So that Bellimante, yeilding to my Implorings, consented next day to go with me to this retreat of Favors.

Accordingly the next morning we set out for this amiable place; where we arrived, and finding myself all alone, without interruption or fear, with this very fair Creature, I advanced to a thousand Freedoms which she, with some resistance, permitted me to take: I was all Joy and Transport at every advance, and still the nearer I approached to the last Favour, the more blest I imagined myself; I grew more resolved, and she more feeble; and at last, I was the Victor and Bellimante the Victim; I remained some days with her, and one would have imagined I should have been intirely happy in this place with one so young and fair: But behold the fickleness of, Youth, and Man's nature.

Thô my Heart were full of Passion,
And I found the yeilding Maid
Give a loose to inclination
While her Love her Flame betray'd;
Yet thô all she did impart,
Pain and Anguish prest my Heart.

Thô I found her all o'r Charming,
Fond and sighing in my Arms;
Yet my Heart anew was warming
For Bellinda's unknown Charms;
Thought, if Beauty pleas'd me so,
What must Wit and Beauty too?

And though next day I found myself a hundred times more in Love with Bellimante than before, yet unless I could possess Bellinda too, I thought myself miserable: Yet every time she charmed me anew I was upon the point of renouncing eternally Bellinda, and sacrificing her to my Passion for Bellimante: But I did not remain long in that Humour, but every day grew more and more unresolved in that point; and as Bellimante grew more fond I grew more cold; not but I had learnt to say so many kind and soft things in the time of my real Passion with Silvia, that I found it easie to speak every day such endearing Words as gave her no doubt of my Heart; nor was willing she should see to the bottom of it, where she would most certainly have found Bellinda; yet with such a mixture of Passion for herself, that it would have been hard to have distinguished, which had had the ascendant there; only my desire at present was the most considerable for the fair Object I had not yet possest, and whom I long'd to vanquish; perhaps, as much for the Glory as the Pleasure, though my Heart did not at this moment think so.

After some time that I had lived here with Bellimante, I made some pretext to leave her for a little while; she, who was extreamly charmed with that Solitude, resolved to wait there my return, so that I had some pain in contriving how I should bring Bellinda to the same Castle as I wished to do; but it had in it many Mansions and Apartments, and, as I said, so retired from one another, that it was difficult to come at any time together or to meet: This consideration made me resolved, and very pressing with Bellinda, to go to this place, assuring her of such Diversion as she never met with in any other part of the World: She loved and was not long in persuading, and I had the Glory to conduct her in spight of all her Wit and Gayety, to this retreat of Solitude with me; where, unperceived, I obliged her to render me all that Love could allow, and more than Honour would permit: And I was for some days extreamly happy, and possibly had continued so, (going from one Apartment to another, and, like the Great Sultan, visiting by turns my Beauties,) had not a malicious fate prevented my Grandeur and Pleasure.

It hap'ned one day that I had sued a repetition of Favours from Bellinda; she seeming resolved to grant me no more, repenting of those I had taken, and with a charming Sorrow reproaching me, making me a thousand times more pressing than before: At last her force growing weaker, her denials fainter, and my importunities more raging; I found her yeilding, the Lily in her Face gave place to the Roses, and Love and Trembling made her Eyes more fair, and just ready to render me all. We saw approaching us Bellimante, who, having heard how I sometimes past my hours, resolved to surprise me in my perfidy; and accordingly found us in a gloomy Arbour with all the Transports of Love in both our Faces, which it was too late to resettle and hide from this too sensible and jealous fair One: In vain I strove with all the Arguments of Love and Tenderness to appease her, or, if by anything I said, I found her inclined to pardon me, on the other side it but served to incense and enrage Bellinda, to whom I had made equal Vows (at her coming to that place,) of eternal Fidelity. I am not able to express to you, my dear Lysander, what confusion I found myself in, I divided my Heart and my Entreaties between 'em; and knew not to which I most ardently meant 'em; I was very sensible, that while I treated both with equal Love and Respect, that I should gain neither, and yet if what I said to both had been addrest to any one of 'em, it would have prevailed; and I found it easie to have kept either, if I would resolve to quit the other; but my heart not inclining to that, or if it wou'd, not knowing which I shou'd chuse, made me remain between 'em both the most out-of-countenanced coxcomb, that ever was taken in the cheats of Love, while both were on either side reproaching me with all the malice and noise imaginable, so that not being able longer to endure the clamour, I took my flight from 'em both, and ran with all the force I cou'd to a Village call'd Irresolution; and where Coquet Love abandon'd me saying that place was not proper for him.

The Houses of this Village are for the most part not half built, but all appears very desolate and ruinous: It appertains to a Lady very fantastique of the same name. She makes a Figure pleasant enough, she never dresses herself, because she cannot determin what habit to put on; she is ever tormenting herself, still turning to this side and to that, yet never stirs from the place, because undetermin'd she knows not whither nor which way to go: And having so many in her mind resolves to go to neither; one always sees an Agitation in her Eyes, that keeps them in perpetual motion and fixt on nothing. You see her perpetually perplext with a thousand designs in her head at once, but puts none of them in execution.

I found myself in this place Embarrassed with a thousand confusions and thoughts, for Bellinda and Bellimante had equally shar'd my soul, and I knew not for which I shou'd declare; nor whether the Wit and extream good Humour of the first were more powerful upon my heart, than the Beauty and softness of the last, so that I was wholly unable to determin which I shou'd quit, having the same sentiments for one as the other, and resolv'd to abandon both rather than content myself with one: And the fear of losing one was the occasion of my losing both, in fine I was in the most cruel incertainty in the World. And I cou'd not forbear saying a thousand times to myself,

When Love shall two fair objects mix,
And in the Heart two passions fix:
'Tis a pleasure too severe,
Cruel Joy we cannot bear,
Too much Love for two I own,
But too little flame for one.

While I was thus perplext betwixt these two violent passions, when no reason cou'd resolve me which to choose, as I was one day meditating what to do in this extremity, a Woman presented herself to me, whose Beauty was infinitely transcending all I had ever beheld; she had a noble and Majestick meen, a most Divine Air, and her charms cast so great a Lustre that I was dazzl'd with Gazing on her; she struck me with so profound a respect at the first sight of her Glory's, that I cou'd not forbear throwing myself at her feet, imploring I might be eternally permitted to Adore her; and to become her slave. When raising me from the ground, and looking on me with Eyes more Majestick than kind, she said to me in a loud voyce:

Fly, Lysidus, this hated Place,
Too long thou'st bin a slave to Love.
Thy youth has yet a nobler Race
In more Illustrious paths to move.
Glory your fonder flame controuls,
Glory, the life of generous Souls.

Once you must Love to learn to live,
'Tis the first lesson you shou'd learn;
Useful instructions Love will give,
If you avoid too much concern:
Loves flame, thô in appearance bright,
Deceives with false and glittering light.

But, Lysidus, the time is come
You must to Beauty bid adieu;
Recal your wandering passions home.
And only be to Glory true;
She is a Mistress that will last
When all Loves fires are gone and past.

Those words, repeated to me with an Air haughty and imperious, toucht me to the very Soul, and made me blush a thousand times with shame to behold myself in that ridiculous state, almost reduc'd to the same tenderness for Bellinda and Bellimante I had before had for Silvia; but I soon found my error and in an instant became more in Love with Glory than I had ever been in my life. Insomuch that I resolv'd to leave Irresolution and follow her. I confess at first it gave my heart som little pain to withdraw and disingage it from so long and so fond a custom, and I was more than once forc'd to parley thus with my intractable and stubborn heart.

Oh! fond remembrance! do not bring
False notions to my easy heart.
And make the foolish tender thing
Think, that with Love it cannot part;
Or dy when er'e the charming God
Forsak's his old and kind abode.

And thou, my heart, be calm and Pleas'd,
For better hours thou now shalt see,
Of all thy Anxious torments eas'd
From all thy toyles and slavery free,
From Beauties Pride and peevish scorns,
From Wits Intregueing false returns.

'Tis Honour now thou shalt persue,

Her dictates only shalt obey;
Yet Beauty en Passant may view
And be with all loves Pleasures Gay,
Quench when you please resistless fires,
But make no business of desires.

Thus, my dear Lysander, following Glory, I soon arriv'd at the extent of the Island of Love, and there I incounter'd a thousand Beauties, Attractions, Graces and Agreements; all which endeavor'd anew, but in vain, to engage me. I past by 'em all without any regard only sight, as I beheld 'em with the remembrance, how once the meanest of those Beauties wou'd have charm'd me. I lookt back on all those happy shades, who had been conscious of my softest pleasures, and a thousand times I sighing bid 'em farewell; the Rivers, Springs and Fountains had my wishes that they might still be true and favor Lovers, as they had a thousand times done me. These dear remembrance, you may believe, stay'd some time with me, yet I wou'd not for an Empire have return'd to 'em again, nor have liv'd that life over anew I had so long and with so much pleasure persu'd.

After this I took a Vessel and put off from that shore, where, thô I had met with many Misfortunes, I had also receiv'd a thousand joys: While it was in view I found myself toucht with some regret, but being sail'd out of sight of it, I sigh'd no more, but bid adieu to fond Love for ever.

All you Beauties and Attractions,
That make so many hearts submit;
Soft inspirers of affection,
Mistresses of dear bought wit;
To whose Empire we resigning
Prove our homage justly due,
After all our sighs and whining
Dear delight we bid adieu.

After all your fond Caprices,
All your Arts to seem Divine,
Painting, Patching and your Dresses,
Easy votaryes to incline;
After all your couzening Billets,
Sighs and tears, but all untrue,
To your Gilting tricks and quillets,
I for ever bid adieu.

APHRA BEHN – A SHORT BIOGRAPHY

Aphra Behn was baptised on December 14th in 1640.

Although she was a prolific and well established writer in her own lifetime facts about her remain scant and difficult to confirm. What can safely be said though is that Aphra Behn is now regarded as a key English playwright and a major figure in Restoration theatre

In fact even where and to whom she was born are subject to discussion.

According to which account you read – and there are many – Aphra was born in Harbledown, near Canterbury. Another that she was born to a barber, John Amis and his wife Amy. Or again she was born to a couple named Cooper.

In the "The Histories And Novels of the Late Ingenious Mrs. Behn" (1696) it is written that Aphra was born to Bartholomew Johnson, a barber, and Elizabeth Denham, a wet-nurse. However a claim by Colonel Thomas Colepeper, who states he knew her as a child, wrote in Adversaria that she was born at "Sturry or Canterbury" to a Mr Johnson and that she had a sister named Frances. Anne Kingsmill Finch, Countess of Winchilsea, a poetic contemporary, says that Aphra was born in Wye in Kent, and was the 'Daughter to a Barber.'

None of these accounts can be relied upon and it follows that with so few facts the early part of her life cannot be clearly illustrated.

However what can be accurately suggested is that Aphra was born in the rising tensions to the English Civil War. Obviously a time of much division and difficulty as the King and Parliament, and their respective forces, came ever closer to conflict.

But still facts do not reveal themselves in any quantity. As a young woman a version exists of Aphra's journeying to Surinam with Bartholomew Johnson. He was said to have died on the journey, leaving his wife and children spending some months in the country. It is during this trip that Aphra claims to have met an African slave leader. These experiences formed the basis for one of her most famous works, "Oroonoko". In "Oroonoko" Behn Aphra gifts herself the position of narrator and her first biographer accepted the proposition that Aphra was indeed the daughter of the lieutenant general of Surinam, as in the story. There is little evidence to support this case, and none of her contemporaries acknowledge this, or any, aristocratic status. There is also no evidence that Oroonoko existed as an actual person or that any such slave revolt, is anything but an invention.

However it is possible that she acted a spy in the colony. Possibilities exist. Perhaps Aphra re-wrote her own history as and when it suited her needs at the time.

The common method of gathering information in these times was Church records and for a few, tax records. Aphra Behn is mentioned in neither. As well as Aphra Behn or Mrs Behn she was, at times, also known as Ann Behn, Mrs Bean, agent 160 and Astrea.

Shortly after her supposed return to England from Surinam in 1664, Aphra may have married Johan Behn (also written as Johann and John Behn). He could have been a merchant of German or Dutch extraction, possibly from Hamburg. He died or the couple separated that same year, however from this point we can be sure Aphra used the title "Mrs Behn" as her professional name.

There is some suggestion that Aphra may have been a Catholic or at least leaned towards this school of faith. She once commented that she was "designed for a nun." Many of those around her were Catholic, such as Henry Neville who was later arrested for his Catholicism, and this would have aroused suspicions during the anti-Catholic fervour of the 1680s. She was a monarchist, and her sympathy for the Stuarts, and particularly for the Catholic Duke of York may be demonstrated by her dedication of her play "The

Rover, Part II" to him after he had been exiled for the second time. Aphra was dedicated to the restored King Charles II. As political parties emerged during this time, Aphra became a Tory supporter.

By 1666 Aphra had become attached to the court. Domestically the Plague was sweeping the Nation and the Great Fire was about to erupt through London. In foreign affairs England and the Netherlands had engaged in The Second Anglo-Dutch War from 1665. Aphra was recruited as a political spy in Antwerp on behalf of King Charles II, possibly in league with Thomas Killigrew.

This is probably the beginning of more accurate records on Aphra's life. Her code name is said to have been Astrea (though there are others), a name under which she later published many of her writings. Her chief duty was to establish a relationship with William Scot, son of Thomas Scot, a regicide who had been executed in 1660. Scot was believed to be ready to become a spy in the English service and to report on the activities of the English exiles who were thought to be plotting against the King. Aphra arrived in Bruges in July 1666 with a mission to secure Scot into a double agent, but there is evidence that Scot would betray her to the Dutch.

Aphra however found life as a spy not quite the romantic interlude that many assume would be the case. She arrived unprepared; the cost of living shocked her, and after a month, she had to pawn her jewellery. King Charles was slow in paying, either for her services or for her expenses whilst abroad. She had to borrow money so she could return to London, where she spent a year petitioning King Charles for payment unsuccessfully. A short while later a warrant was issued for her arrest, but little to suggest it was actually served or that she went to prison for her debt.

The death of her husband and her debts seemed to push her towards a more sustainable and substantial career. Aphra began work for the King's Company and the Duke's Company players as a scribe. These were, in fact, the only two licensed theatre groups in London. The theatres had been closed under Cromwell and were now re-opening under Charles II and a more liberal atmosphere. Theatre technology was being imported from Europe and being integrated into the staging of some plays. It was a great moment on which to embark upon a career in theatre.

Aphra who had previously only written poetry now embarked on such a career. Her first, "The Forc'd Marriage", was staged in 1670, followed by "The Amorous Prince" (1671). After her third play, "The Dutch Lover", fails to please Aphra had a three year lull in her writing career. Again it is speculated that she went travelling again, possibly once again as a spy.

After this sojourn her writing moves towards comic works, which prove commercially more successful. Her most popular works included "The Rover" and "Love-Letters Between a Nobleman and His Sister" (1684–87).

With her growing reputation Aphra became friends with many of the most notable writers of the day. This is The Age of Dryden and his literary dominance. As well as his friendship she includes also those of Elizabeth Barry, John Hoyle, Thomas Otway and Edward Ravenscroft, and was also attached to the circle of the Earl of Rochester.

Aphra often used her plays to attack the parliamentary Whigs claiming, "In public spirits call'd, good o' th' Commonwealth... So tho' by different ways the fever seize...in all 'tis one and the same mad disease." This was Aphra's criticism to parliament which had denied the king funds.

From the mid 1680's Aphra's health began to decline. This was exacerbated by her continual state of debt and descent into poverty.

In 1687 she published A Discovery of New Worlds, a translation of a French popularisation of astronomy, Entretiens sur la pluralité des mondes, by Bernard le Bovier de Fontenelle, written as a novel in a form similar to her own work, but with her new, religiously oriented preface.

As her end approached in 1689 it became increasingly hard for her to even hold a pen though her desire to continue to write was unquenchable. In her final days, she wrote the translation of the final book of Abraham Cowley's Six Books of Plants.

Aphra Behn died on April 16th 1689, and is buried in the East Cloister of Westminster Abbey. The inscription on her tombstone reads: "Here lies a Proof that Wit can never be Defence enough against Mortality." She was quoted as stating that she had led a "life dedicated to pleasure and poetry."

Her legacy is broad. Firstly as a woman she broke down many of the barriers which regarded only men as writers, especially in the commercial arena. In all she would write and have performed 19 plays, contribute to more, and become one of the first prolific, high-profile female dramatists in these Isles.

In her own golden age of the 1670s and 1680s she was one of the most productive playwrights in Britain, second only to the immense talents of the Poet Laureate John Dryden.

Much of her work has been criticised for its bawdy tone as well as its masculine form but needs must and she was working to live, to survive, and to widen her spread as an author.

She received widespread support from many other successful writers including Thomas Otway, Nahum Tate (also a Poet Laureate), Jacob Tonson, Nathaniel Lee and Thomas Creech.

Aphra is now rightly seen as a key dramatist of the seventeenth-century theatre. Her prose vitally important to the on-going development of the English novel.

Following Aphra's death new female dramatists such as 'Ariadne', Delarivier Manley, Mary Fix, Susanna Centlivre and Catherine Trotter acknowledged Behn as an inspiration who opened up the public space for women writers to be accepted.

In succeeding centuries her appreciation has been volatile. For instance in the morally reserved Victorian clime both the writer and her works were ignored or dismissed as indecent. The Victorian novelist and critic Julia Kavanagh wrote, "the disgrace of Aphra Behn is that, instead of raising man to woman's moral standard, she sank woman to the level of man's coarseness".

However by the 20th century, however, Aphra's fame was back in fashion. Since then her works have been well appreciated and her place in our literary pantheon assured.

APHRA BEHN – A CONCISE BIBLIOGRAPHY

Plays

The Forced Marriage (1670)
The Amorous Prince (1671)
The Dutch Lover (1673)
Abdelazer (1676)
The Town Fop (1676)
The Rover, Part I (1677)
Sir Patient Fancy (1678)
The Feigned Courtesans (1679)
The Young King (1679)
The False Count (1681)
The Rover, Part II (1681)
The Roundheads (1681)
The City Heiress (1682)
Like Father, Like Son (1682)
Prologue and Epilogue to Romulus and Hersilia, or The Sabine War (November 1682)
The Lucky Chance (1686) with composer John Blow
The Emperor of the Moon (1687)
The Widow Ranter (1689)
The Younger Brother (1696)

Novels
The Fair Jilt
Agnes de Castro
Love-Letters Between a Nobleman and His Sister (1684)
Oroonoko (1688)

Short Stories
The Fair Jilt (1688)
The History of the Nun: or, the Fair Vow-Breaker (1688)
The History of the Servant
The Lover-Boy of Germany
The Girl Who Loved the German Lover-Boy

Poetry Collections
Poems upon Several Occasions, with A Voyage to the Island of Love (1684)
Lycidus; or, The Lover in Fashion (1688)

www.ingramcontent.com/pod-product-compliance
Lightning Source LLC
Chambersburg PA
CBHW060139050426
42448CB00010B/2213